FOOTBALL BUSINESS

How markets are breaking
the beautiful game

☉ ☉ ☉

TSJALLE VAN DER BURG

infinite ideas

First published in 2014 by
Infinite Ideas Limited
36 St Giles
Oxford
OX1 3LD
United Kingdom
www.infideas.com

A CIP catalogue record for this book is available from the British Library.

ISBN 978-1-908984-27-2

Designed and typeset by GRID.

Printed in Britain.

CONTENTS

CONTENTS

Online supplement available at www.infideas.com/football-business-supplement.

INTRODUCTION

'Go out and enjoy the game'. These were the words the legendary Bill Shankly used when sending his team on to the field. He did not say this because he was concerned about his players having a pleasant Saturday afternoon. He said it because he knew his men would play better if they enjoyed their work on the field.

Many people say they don't like economics. They say it's too difficult. But in conversations with football fans who are concerned about the financial problems of their club, or about other problems in football, I have noticed that people can understand all kinds of economic principles once they are really interested. So I think football fans will be able to understand this book. At least, if I tell the story well. I will do my best.

The book is about the economic problems that currently exist in European club football, or may emerge in its future, and the possibilities for solving or preventing them. The book itself discusses this subject in a simple way, but there is also a supplement that provides, for interested readers who have more time to spend, a full scientific background.* Readers who just want to understand the main ideas do not need to refer to the supplement.

We need to warm up before turning to the main subject. Thus, we start with some stories about the history of football. These stories have some relevance for the discussion later on, but the main thing is to stay relaxed. The warm-up ends with some remarks about the 'rules of the game' used in this book – and then we are ready to go out and face the problems of modern-day football. I hope you enjoy the game.

* See the online supplement at www.infideas.com/football-business-supplement

1

MADE IN THE PAST

EUROPEAN NOT-FOR-PROFIT ORGANIZATIONS

They were not like those ambitious, modern students who dream of founding their own multi-million company before they are thirty. No, they were not. Nathaniel Creswick and William Prest were different. When the two young men founded, on 24 October 1857, the first football club ever, they were not thinking of money. Sheffield FC was intended for fun.

The club was an instant success. In the years before, games that were a lot like football had been played in the streets, on fields and in school playgrounds. So the new football club tapped into something big. Other clubs soon followed, as did a national Football Association, which launched a cup competition for England in 1871 – the FA Cup Tournament. The new sport also attracted a lot of spectators. In 1892, for instance, 25,000 people watched West Bromwich Albion win the Cup Final against Aston Villa 3–0. By that time, some of the players were being paid, which was officially permitted.

In the beginning, the football clubs were voluntary organizations consisting of voting members and run by committees. But for the bigger clubs this soon proved unsatisfactory. They needed to borrow large sums of money in order to build large stands. Club directors had to stand surety for those loans, which meant they would have to stump up the money themselves if the club was unable to pay back the loan. That became too much of a risk. For this reason, in the period up to 1920, nearly all the clubs in the higher divisions were converted into limited companies with shareholders – because shareholders are not liable for the company's debts if it goes bust. The first shareholders paid the club money in return for their shares to enable the club to invest. Those shares later entitled them to dividends. But the football clubs introduced a rule not known in other companies: there was a maximum for the dividends, and that maximum was fairly low. And actual dividends were on average lower still; in many cases, no dividends were paid at all. One did not become a shareholder to get rich from a club's profits. In this way, until around 1980, almost all clubs basically remained not-for-profit organizations.

What were the motives of the board members? Many were football enthusiasts who wanted to see their team win on the field and who liked to contribute to the fans' happiness. Some were also motivated by the idea that the club had a positive effect on society more generally. And, of course, no director objected when his reputation was enhanced by association with the club. To be sure, there were also directors who used a club to promote their own business interests. After all, building a stadium was good business, and private companies could earn money through clubs in other ways too. Still, for most board members, such indirect profit motives were absent or, in any case, not predominant.

Elsewhere in Europe comparable developments took place, albeit at a slower pace. For example, professional football began in France in 1932, and in the Netherlands as late as 1954. Each country had its own legal system which led to differences in organizational forms. For instance, some Dutch clubs were converted to foundations after the advent of professional football. In France the clubs remained associations of citizens for many decades, with local government being involved in the financing and administration of the clubs. This often included municipal ownership of the stadium. In quite a number of other countries such forms of government involvement were less important or did not exist at all. But one thing was the same everywhere in Europe: until 1980 almost no club was primarily interested in profit. The main aim was to offer people an enjoyable form of recreation.

As such, it was not-for-profit organizations that made not only amateur football but also professional football. The pleasure derived from top-level football by tens of millions of television viewers and spectators before 1980 was basically down to the not-for-profit sector. This sector made a fantastic contribution to society.

Around 1980 the scene started to change somewhat. Since then quite a few European clubs have come into the hands of new owners who have the statutory right to use the club to make profits for themselves. To what extent they use this opportunity is a question for later.

A question for now is this: what would have happened if, back in 1980, the European authorities had stipulated that all football clubs must basically keep their traditional ownership structure? Part of the answer can be given here. Even without the new types of owners the stands would be well filled and the final of the top European cup competition would attract millions of viewers. Certainly clubs that now have rich owners, such as Chelsea, would not stand as good a chance of reaching the final, or even winning it. This is a shame for Chelsea fans, but it is also great news for other supporters. After all, a cup final is always between two clubs and only one can be the winner. That was true in 1872 and it is still true today.

AMERICAN ENTREPRENEURS

Whereas Europe experienced the rise of football in the nineteenth century, in the United States it was baseball that became popular. Baseball had an early start. It has been said that Rochester, New York, already had a baseball club in 1825. It had fifty members aged between eighteen and forty years old, who played the game during the afternoon. Over the next forty years many other clubs emerged. As in European football these early clubs were associations run by volunteers.

Around 1867, however, the entrepreneur appeared on the scene. Soon most of the better teams were owned by individuals who used the team to make a living, if not a tidy profit. Other top teams were owned by commercial companies. The entrepreneurial model was successful in increasing attendances. As early as 1869 the Cincinnati Red Stockings sometimes played in front of 10,000 paying spectators. The club also paid all its players a salary that year. No English football club had yet reached that point. In 1871 a national baseball league was set up in the United States.

One prominent owner was saloon-keeper Chris von der Ahe from St Louis. In 1881 he noticed that drinking establishments close to the ground of the local baseball team, the Brown Stockings, sold a lot of beer on match days. That inspired him. He bought the baseball club and built an amusement park with music, horse racing and a beer garden next to the ground. His entrepreneurial spirit inspired other club owners, and since then there have been many and varied entertainments on offer around the summertime baseball games.

Since those days there have been many club owners who were motivated by the opportunity of making a profit from their club. Sometimes a club owner also owned another business, such as a broadcasting company, which benefited from profitable contracts awarded by the club. However, non-financial motives have also played an important role. Quite a number of owners were sportsmen who just liked to win. Others were just happy to be in the spotlight. In relation to such motives, many owners bought more top players than was actually good for profits. There were also men who regarded their ownership of the local team as a civic duty and who were interested in broader issues. For instance, owner of the Chicago Cubs, Phil Wrigley, did not allow night games in his park until 1988 because he did not want night-time noise and traffic in the neighbourhood. However, for most owners, profits were the primary motive and many did well in financial terms – although, as in any business, there were also losses from time to time.

A baseball club needs rivals to play against. But an entrepreneur prefers to have as few rivals as possible, because it means higher sales at higher prices, and also less competition for the better players. So in 1876, a small number of clubs formed a national league with the rule that new clubs would only be permitted to join with the agreement of the existing participants. As a result only a few more teams would later join. They also agreed that there would be no relegation. After all, an entrepreneur would rather not risk losing income due to something as unpredictable as that.

This old model still exists today. The national league competition, Major League Baseball, currently includes thirty clubs. An umbrella organization runs the league competition and sells the broadcasting rights to national TV stations. This generates a lot of money, which the clubs split between them. With the exception of New York, no city has more than one club in the Major League. This gives each club a monopoly within its city and far beyond. As a result, the club can demand high prices for tickets, merchandising and TV rights for regional broadcasters. Similar models exist in American football and basketball, sports which became popular later.

A club in the highest league can move cities, which happens now and again. A city that offers big subsidies for a new stadium stands a good chance of getting a club, or keeping the ones they have. This can cost the city hundreds of millions of dollars. The owners win and the taxpayer is the loser – especially if he or she doesn't like professional sport.

But sports fans can suffer too, as fans of the Baltimore Colts discovered for themselves. The Colts played in Baltimore for years, winning many honours. They even won the Super Bowl. The club was much loved – rarely, so Americans say, has there been a bond between a club and its supporters like the one between the Colts and the people of Baltimore. All of this came to an end one sad night in March 1984.

That evening hardly anyone knew what was about to happen. In the middle of the night, on the instructions of owner Bob Irsay, removal lorries rolled up to take away the contents of the stadium and move them to Indianapolis, where the team would play on under a different name. When Baltimore awoke the next morning it no longer had a football club. Arriving at the stadium members of staff saw to their bewilderment that almost everything had gone, from the office furniture to the dumb-bells. Years later Baltimore had still not recovered from the blow. On the streets you would see banners pleading, 'Give Baltimore the ball'.

Yes, entrepreneurship has its advantages, but it also has its drawbacks.

THE 1960 ALL-SPORTS WORLD SERIES

The moment came on 13 October 1960, at Forbes Field in Pittsburgh. During the seventh game of the World Series between the Pittsburgh Pirates and the New York Yankees, Bill Mazeroski hit a ninth-inning home run, winning the game for the Pirates 10–9 and their first World Championship since 1925. The 37,000-strong crowd erupted in a wild celebration, while the famous Yankees stood in disbelief. More than fifty years later fans still gather annually on the remnants of the old ball park to celebrate the anniversary of that legendary home run. And many Americans consider the Mazeroski game to be the greatest game of all time. Are they right?

On 18 May of that same year, a 128,000-strong crowd at Glasgow's Hampden Park saw Eintracht Frankfurt take the lead in the European Cup Final against Real Madrid. But, after 30 minutes of play, the time had come for Ferenc Puskás and Alfredo Di Stéfano to show off their superb skills in one of the best football demonstrations ever. Puskás scored four goals and Di Stéfano three, resulting in Real winning the game 7–3. During the entire history of the European Cup and Champions League finals, only four hat-tricks have been scored, and two of them were seen on that wonderful evening at Hampden Park. The usually careful newspaper, *The Times*, commented: 'Real Madrid, with its brilliant performance on Scottish soil, has maintained the suggestion that it is the best team in the world'. But was *The Times* sufficiently careful?

It would have been great if, in that golden year, Real Madrid had played the Pittsburgh Pirates in an All-Sports World Series, but due to some annoying differences in rules this was impossible. Now we will never know which team really was the best.

Fortunately, it still is possible to have a contest between American baseball and European football on the field of economics. The golden sports year of 1960 is a good example for such a contest. Each of the two sports had been in existence for over a century, so it is not a question of young talent versus experienced professionals here. So which sport was performing best?

The English first division, which at that time numbered twenty-two clubs, attracted some 14 million spectators in the 1959–60 season. This corresponded to an average of 31,000 spectators per match. Seventy clubs played in the three divisions below, and 18 million people came through the turnstiles to watch them. In total, the top four divisions in England attracted 32 million spectators – not including the popular cup games. Elsewhere in Europe, the grounds were respectably full too.

In the United States Major League Baseball, which at that time numbered sixteen clubs, attracted some 20 million spectators in the 1960 season – more than the English first division, in other words. But the average number of spectators per match was lower: 16,000. This reflected the fact that a baseball club played more than 150 matches per year. In Minor League Baseball there were 155 clubs overall and a total of 11 million people paid to watch them. Added together, Major League and Minor League attracted 31 million spectators. That is slightly fewer than the 32 million for the top four English divisions. At that time American football and basketball were not yet very popular;

the top leagues of these two sports together attracted fewer than 5 million spectators.

Essentially, there were no more spectators in the United States than in England, whereas the United States did have four times the population; so the number of spectators per head of population in England was several times higher. The picture is similar when other European countries are included in the comparison, leaving only one possible conclusion: European football attracted many more spectators than baseball.

Moreover, European sports fans paid comparatively little. For instance, the average ticket for a match in the English first division cost fourteen pence at 1960 prices while the average ticket for a Major League Baseball game was around one dollar and ninety cents. Taking into account the different values of the pound and the dollar, this meant that a baseball match would have set you back about three-and-a-half times as much as a football match.

All in all, from the perspective of the sports fan, European football did much better than American baseball. Indeed, if all fans of professional team sports in 1960 had been asked whether Real Madrid or the Pittsburgh Pirates were the better team, in all likelihood the majority would have declared Real the winner.

THE 'THIRD HALF'

Now that the game is over the whistle for the third half can be blown. We still need to explain why the Americans lost and the Europeans won. To begin with the American entrepreneurs simply had bad luck. Let us be honest here. Baseball, the sport inherited by the entrepreneurs in about 1867 from the voluntary organizations, just happens to be more boring. Players stay in the same position most of the time. Unexpected actions are rarely seen and there is little room for genius.

Perhaps baseball fans may not agree, but everyone can give his opinion in the third half and this happens to be mine.

Whatever Americans may think of my opinion, the fact is that there is no scientific evidence that it is not true. Experienced third-half players will find it easy to put forward various other good ideas to explain why the Americans lost. The reasons may be speculative but, nevertheless, may hold some truth. Indeed, there are many things we do not know for certain and so a complete scientific explanation for the American defeat is out of reach. This being said, some other reasons for the defeat will be discussed below.

To begin with it is not speculation to say that the high prices charged by American team owners had a negative impact on attendance. In this case the entrepreneurs were fully to blame. They created a closed league with a small number of clubs. Major League Baseball had only sixteen clubs in 1960 and they were dispersed widely over the country, with no town having two clubs. So no team had competitors located nearby. And, according to accepted economic principles, firms aiming for profits charge higher prices when they have fewer competitors.

On the other side of the pond the smaller country of England had a system of promotion and relegation in which many different clubs could play in the top division – at least occasionally. As a result, the average English club faced more serious competition from clubs nearby. Consequently, there was a bigger chance that the stadium would be empty if ticket prices were too high. This is one of the reasons why English ticket prices were lower than ticket prices in the United States.

Another, possibly more important, reason for low ticket prices was that the English clubs were not aiming to make a profit but had other objectives, among which were social concerns. Exploiting the fans was not regarded as socially acceptable. So, as long as the costs of running the clubs remained low, the clubs had a good reason to avoid high ticket prices.

And costs were low indeed. The English clubs had low wage-bills. From 1901 the clubs had a maximum wage for players (which was abolished in 1961). In 1960 this maximum was about one-and-a-half times the wage of an industrial labourer. There was also a strict transfer system: when a player wanted to move to another club, his club had the right to charge a transfer fee, even if the player's contract had expired. This weakened his negotiating position, which further contributed to low wages. Low costs made low ticket prices possible.

In the United States there was also a (special kind of) transfer system, which was also strict and prevented wages from skyrocketing. But the American system had been introduced especially with the aim of increasing profits, and so it did not lead to lower ticket prices.

All in all, the main reason for the higher ticket prices in the United States was that the club owners wanted to make money and had created a closed league system which helped to realize that goal. These higher ticket prices are at least one of the reasons for the lower attendances at matches in the US.

Despite the high ticket prices, the American sports model, with its entrepreneurs, suited American culture, by and large. The Americans always understood that entrepreneurs wanted to make money. Indeed, a good entrepreneur was fulfilling 'the American Dream', that wonderful ideal of shoeshine boys who can become millionaires by seizing opportunities and working hard in the 'Land of the Free'. And if, thanks to such entrepreneurs, many people got to enjoy baseball, it was also reasonable that they should be asked to pay for it. Of course, the supporters were not always satisfied, especially if their club moved to a different city. But essentially the entrepreneurial model suited American culture.

And the European sports model suited European culture. Associations had traditionally been important. Anyone who wanted to play football could join an amateur club. Professional football grew out of amateur football and long remained connected with it. Young players usually came under the care of a youth coach at an amateur club. Was it right that this coach should have to pay high prices to watch a professional match which might feature one of his former pupils? Football owed its success to the efforts of volunteers. Viewed in that way it was only reasonable that tickets should be cheap. Throughout Europe low prices and packed stands reflected a culture marked by a certain solidarity.

Europeans have more in common than they sometimes think.

OLD SOLDIERS NEVER DIE

In Europe professional football has given pleasure to a great many fans for more than a century now. But, despite its popularity, it has witnessed financial troubles throughout its history. For instance, many English clubs had monetary problems during the Great Depression of the 1930s, and a couple of clubs went out of existence at that time.

Focusing on the last fifty years we see that the English clubs had especially bad times in the 1980s, when they encountered a fundamental crisis in terms of debts, mismanagement, stadium disasters, hooliganism and poor attendance levels. In France, the period between 1969 and 1974 was a particularly bad one, with many clubs in danger and a number of bankruptcies. And between 1982 and 1994 there was another period of financial deficits, augmented by corruption offences. Similar tales can be told about other European countries.

How can these problems be explained? Since the beginning of professional football the situation for the clubs has been as follows. In order to please the fans, and directors who are sportsmen, the team has to win. To do so it needs good players. Good players can be costly in terms of wages, transfer fees and the costs of training and youth development. Therefore, it is important to earn money.

To earn money it is crucial to have successes on the field. This increased the number of paying spectators. In more recent times it has also increases the number of television viewers and, in turn, the revenues from broadcasting. Successes on the field and large audiences also have positive effects on the revenues from merchandising and the contributions from sponsors and advertisers. Therefore, to a large extent, revenues depend on playing success. And this means that there is also a financial motive for spending large sums of money on players.

However, if through misfortune or other causes the team loses a lot of matches, revenues will fall. This in turn will reduce the chances of securing good players and doing well on the pitch. In this way, a vicious circle is created, which some clubs have found themselves unable to get out of, causing them to lose touch with the top divisions for years – or forever. But even clubs that have not done badly on the pitch have had financial problems now and then, the reason being that spending on players was very high, while the big successes and revenues hoped for did not fully materialize.

Of course, mismanagement has also played a role. There is no industry which has not seen bad managers, and football is no exception. On the contrary, it is a business where emotions, publicity and prestige are important and this has had a negative impact on the quality of management in some cases. On the other hand, there have also been directors who have put a great deal of effort into their clubs, taken sensible initiatives to increase revenues, hired good coaches and players without spending too much, and made their clubs very successful.

Indeed, history has seen many failures, but it has seen many successful clubs too.

Despite the fact that many clubs have had big financial problems, the existence of large clubs has been safe in most cases. All the big European clubs that existed in 1960 still exist today. And many of the small clubs with serious financial problems have also been able to survive, although some small clubs have had to leave the scene. Why do so many troubled clubs survive?

In industries outside football it is normal to witness the disappearance of a company now and then. Life goes on. For instance, when a dairy goes bankrupt its customers simply turn to another milk producer. But when a football club disappears there is no good substitute for its fans and this creates a problem. Therefore, history has witnessed many efforts to save failing clubs.

Such efforts have taken different forms. Some clubs have been rescued by sponsors, others by investors who obtained an ownership stake. In many countries local governments have rescued clubs. Some insolvent clubs have let their creditors agree on a reduction of their claims, sometimes under the threat of liquidation which would hurt the creditors even more. And some clubs have been liquidated but have re-formed soon after. This basically means that the club moves on without its old debts in the form of a 'phoenix club' with a slightly different name. In this way the creditors lose their claims. For the club the main disadvantage can be that, depending on the rules of the football association, it has to make its new start in a much lower league, because it has lost its old licence to play. But in any case, the club continues to exist.

In 1961 the Italian club Fiorentina won the final of the European Cup Winners' Cup, beating Glasgow Rangers 4–1 over two matches. Fortunately, Rangers managed to win the same cup eleven years later.

In 2002 Fiorentina went bankrupt. Its assets were immediately bought by a new phoenix club called Florentia Viola in 2002 and called ACF Fiorentina since 2003 (when the club bought back its old name). The new club had to start three divisions lower, so it took some years to get back to the highest level. This was the chance for Rangers to prove they were the better club after all. And they did. They managed to exist for a further ten years, winning five Scottish titles during that time. It was only as late as 2012 that Rangers became bankrupt. In Glasgow there is also a phoenix club now, called Rangers FC. Old soldiers never die.

RULES OF THE GAME

The old days have gone. The time has come to turn to the real subject of this book: the economic problems that currently exist in European club football and those that may emerge in its future. The book is meant to be accessible for all kinds of readers. At the same time, parts of it meet scientific standards. In these parts, the main line of argument is given in the book itself, while the more detailed background information, which scientists require, is available in the online supplement. Readers with little time to spare are advised to ignore the supplement.

Where does the book meet the scientific standards? We have come to the rules of the game. It may not be a fascinating subject but the rules must be made clear.

Scientific standards are met whenever the book deals with economic questions, specifically the following four. First, what are the economic developments that occur or have occurred in football, how can they be explained and what could be the future economic developments? Second, what are the effects of these developments on the well-being of specific groups of people such as fans, players, club owners or taxpayers? Third, are there any policy measures which can improve the well-being of some of these groups? And fourth, what are the effects of the developments and policy measures on economic welfare?

This brings us to another question. What is economic welfare?

Economic welfare is a central concept in this book. It is the sum total of the well-being of all people in society, or in a country, expressed in terms of money. You may question whether well-being can always be expressed in monetary terms; this is a question for later. At this point, let me give a simple example to demonstrate the main idea.

Consider an investment to improve the comfort of a stadium. Its costs amount to 10 million pounds. They are fully financed through a subsidy, that is, by the taxpayers. This means that the well-being of the taxpayers, expressed in monetary terms, is reduced by 10 million pounds. After all, these people have 10 million pounds less to spend on things that can improve their well-being, such as movies or ice-creams.

Suppose the investment does not draw in larger crowds; the original stadium was sold out anyway. In addition, it does not lead to higher ticket prices. As you see, I am simplifying the problem here. Given this simplification, the only effect on the fans will be that they feel more comfortable in the stadium. This means that their well-being improves. But by how much?

One could ask the fans how much they would be willing to pay for the higher comfort, if they had to pay for it. Suppose the question is asked and all fans give an honest answer. One fan says he is willing to pay 200 pounds (at the most) for the additional comfort over the course of several years; another fan says 320 pounds, and so on. After adding up all the amounts, one finds that the fans are willing to pay 12 million pounds in total. The improvement in well-being of the fans has been expressed in monetary terms as 12 million pounds.

The effects of the investment on economic welfare are equal to the sum total of the effects on the well-being of all the people concerned. The well-being of the fans improves by 12 million pounds; that of the taxpayers is lessened by 10 million pounds. Twelve million minus 10 million is 2 million, so economic welfare improves by 2 million pounds. And an improvement in welfare in itself is a good thing, according to economists.

In a similar way, the effect of any other investment, or any other change, on economic welfare can be analysed.

Economic welfare is a neutral concept, in the sense that it does not matter who benefits and who pays. In the example given above, it is not important whether poor taxpayers mainly paid for luxurious seats for the rich, or whether wealthy taxpayers financed a stadium with standing accommodation only. As far as economic welfare goes, only the sum total of all benefits minus the sum total of all costs matters.

Apart from economic welfare there are many other things that are important for society. For instance, some people will think that it is unfair that taxpayers pay 10 million pounds for the comfort of football fans and object to the subsidy for that reason. Some fans may think differently. Now, it is a task for the government, and for politicians, to deal with such differences in opinion. Economic science has little to contribute here.

This is not to say that issues of fairness will not be discussed. They will, because they are important. However, the point is this: at every place where the book discusses fairness, it is not based on scientific arguments but is just expressing the opinion of the author.

More generally, the book will discuss many questions other than the four economic ones mentioned above. Such questions may concern politics, social relations or other things. Whenever such issues are discussed the text does not (fully) meet the scientific standards. This does not mean the arguments make no sense. After all, science is not the only source of good arguments.

Finally, some readers may come to think that my remarks about Feyenoord, the Rotterdam club, and the club of the people, do not satisfy the academic standards. Let me be frank: all statements concerning the first Dutch club to win the European Cup will be entirely correct. But my choice and assessment of these facts may be biased by emotion. After all, I am a human being and, more importantly, I am a Feyenoord fan.

2

MONEY

DOES MORE MONEY EQUAL MORE ATTRACTIVE PLAY?

What would have happened if Manchester United, the English champions of 2013, had played Burnley, the champions of 1960? The answer is clear: the Mancunians would have beaten the Clarets 158–1. That is, if the score had been expressed in terms of money. The Clarets made 136,000 pounds in 1960 (or, to be precise, in the season ending that year). In that year a pound bought you seventeen times as much as it would in 2013. So 136,000 pounds in 1960 was worth as much as 2.3 million pounds in 2013. However, the Mancunians earned 363 million pounds that year, and this is 158 times as much.

The other English clubs were earning less than the Mancunians in 2013. However, the average Premier League club received, after correcting for inflation, about fifty-three times as much as the average club in the English top division of 1960. Not a bad score. Elsewhere in Europe, professional football has also seen remarkable growth.

It all seems to be a great success. But is it? The revenues of car manufacturers have also exploded since 1960. Consumers spend much more on cars than they used to and they get a lot in return: a wide choice of cars is produced and the cars are of superior quality. Is something similar going on in football?

In football, the quality of the basic product – football matches – has not improved over the years. Barcelona–Real Madrid is no more enjoyable or exciting today than it was in the past. Lionel Messi does not entertain the average Barcelona fan more than Johan Cruijff used to. And in all competitions, fewer goals are scored now. It's a safe bet that in the next final of the Champions League there will not be ten goals in 90 minutes, as there were in the 1960 European Cup final. One of the reasons may be that current coaches put results ahead of entertainment, precisely because of the enormous amounts of money at stake.

From a scientific perspective, a qualification has to be made here. There is no hard evidence as to whether present-day football is no more enjoyable than the football of the past. Indeed, the argument above is merely based on my own, possibly subjective, assessment. Your assessment may well be better than mine.

Still, given my assessment, it is remarkable that present-day fans have to pay much more to enjoy the basic product. Tickets everywhere have become more expensive. And in many countries viewers have to pay for television coverage that used to be free. In addition, many governments help football clubs through subsidies or other means. Quite often the taxpayer foots a large bill, whether he or she likes football or not.

Of course there is some good news too. Today, a lot more people watch football, especially on television. The Premier League is even watched in Asia. There are also more women in the grounds. But this is not so much due to the fact that football clubs are performing better on the pitch. Above all it is down to wider developments in society, such as the rise of television, globalization and the emancipation of women. Of course, the football sector has also made a contribution. For example, stadiums are more comfortable these days, and supporters sometimes get together to organize a great spectacle inside the ground. However, the question remains: why does the fan have to pay so much more?

Most products, if they start selling in greater quantities, will eventually become cheaper. This is because producers benefit from economies of scale, which means that the unit cost of the product falls when more units are sold. In football, however, increased popularity has been associated with higher prices for tickets and television coverage.

Governments sometimes give producers of new products subsidies to help them through a difficult start-up period. But once the business is up and running, and the product is selling well, subsidies normally end. However, in football, governments pay large sums of money to long-existing clubs with skyrocketing revenues.

That makes the football sector unusual. Whereas fans and taxpayers might expect to pay less, they actually pay more.

If clubs are earning so much more money, aren't they making sky-high profits? No. However much clubs earn, they rarely make a profit. If a club's revenues increase, the money is primarily used to buy new players. But all clubs are seeing their revenues rise and they all want better players. This pushes up players' wages and so eliminates most profits. Sometimes clubs buy players who are too expensive, or results on the pitch go against them. So they lose money and governments, creditors, fans or sponsors have to pay the bill.

The positive side of this picture is that players earn high salaries. Good for them, as long as they can deal with the dangers of being rich. Whether their salaries are fair is another question.

All in all, fans and taxpayers are paying a lot of money for a product that is not improving. From their perspective, the performance of club football over recent decades has been decidedly mediocre, compared with, say, the car industry. Could it have been different?

CUTTING YOUR COAT ACCORDING TO YOUR CLOTH

At the start of 2014, the total debt of the clubs in the Spanish Primera División was 3.5 billion euros (about 3 billion pounds). The clubs owed 600 million euros to the government in the form of unpaid taxes. Part of the remaining debt was owed to banks, which were receiving government aid to survive the financial crisis. How the problems of the Spanish clubs are going to be solved remains to be seen, but it is likely that the taxpayer will foot much of the bill.

It is not the first time that taxpayers have been involved in professional football. In Spain, and in a number of other European countries, they have already contributed a great deal of money. In some other countries the government is less inclined to help football clubs. When clubs from such countries get into trouble, other parties pay the price. For example, banks that provide loans and do not get their money back; or other creditors of the club. And of course, there are also losses for the fans of clubs that disappear after a bankruptcy or re-form in a lower league. Yes, the debts of football clubs have many victims.

So how can we put an end to the financial problems in professional football?

In principle, the solution is simple: all clubs should pay their own way. All they have to do is spend less. There are savings to be made, on players in particular. Their wages have risen sharply over the years and could easily be a little lower. And, since many clubs cannot manage to reduce expenditure on their own, they have to be helped from above.

In some countries this is already being done. France has the longest tradition here. In 1991, the French government initiated the National Directorate for Financial Control (DNCG). One of its duties is to control the finances of professional football clubs. To begin with, each club has to present its accounting data to DNCG at specific points in time. When the data show the club is in the red, DNCG normally starts by giving warnings and recommendations. When this does not help, it can block any spending that is contributing to the problem. For instance, payments on transfer fees can be banned. When such directives are ignored more severe sanctions follow and in some cases clubs have even been relegated. All operations and sanctions have been given a solid base in French law. DNCG is independent of the clubs in principle, with the majority of its members being chartered accountants, lawyers and state commissioners. This should make it possible for DNCG to be hard on the clubs – and indeed the system has reduced many financial problems.

The system, however, is not perfect. Some clubs have faked their accounts, thus concealing their precarious financial situation to DNCG. Other clubs have not concealed their deficits, but DNCG has turned a blind eye to them. As a result, some clubs have had to be rescued at a later stage by local governments, sponsors, fans or investors. The availability of such rescue aid leads to what is called a 'soft budget constraint': although a club is not supposed to have big deficits, it can still have them, because when being threatened with bankruptcy it will always get help from outside. DNCG has not been able to harden the budget constraint to a sufficient extent.

These problems have been recognized by the French government and the football authorities, and some improvements have already been made. Three measures for the future are being discussed. The first one addresses the problem that, although DNCG is supposed to be an independent expert body, its members are nominated by representatives of clubs, federations, players and coaches. This means that, ultimately, they may not be fully independent and, as a result, less hard on the clubs. Therefore, the nomination procedure needs to be changed to make the experts fully independent. The second measure is to oblige all clubs to disclose their financial position to the public, so that the media and other parties can help control the clubs. Finally, to prevent clubs from being rescued by governments or investors, budget constraints should be toughened; in other words, rescue packages should no longer be allowed. In conclusion, although control is working, it is not perfect yet – there is room for improvement.

France is not the only country in which the clubs are controlled from above. For instance, the German football authorities also impose financial discipline on the clubs, and this has helped to make the Bundesliga financially stable.

However, not all countries are equally strict. As a result, clubs from countries such as Spain continue to spend substantial amounts of money on players while having big debts. Apart from harming creditors and taxpayers, this also leads to unfair competition in European tournaments. Indeed, there is no fair competition when two clubs which have a debt of more than 500 million euros each, and which both received huge support from their local government, beat all other clubs on their way to the Champions League final, as did Real Madrid and Atlético Madrid in 2014.

We need a European solution.

MICHEL PLATINI AND FINANCIAL FAIR PLAY

Michel Platini is one of the best midfielders in football history and possibly the best free-kick specialist ever. He has won the European Player of the Year Award three times in a row. In 1984 he led France to the title of the European Championship, scoring nine goals in five matches.

But to really reach the ranks of Pelé and Beckenbauer, Platini need-ed to have won the World Cup. In football, winning the highest prize often depends on small things. In 1982 Platini was close to it. With a magnificent French team, he had reached the semi-final of the World Cup in Seville. Their opponents were the tough team of West Ger-many, but Platini's magic, and the artistic skills of the other French stars, led to an exhibition of beauty rarely seen. During the match, any neutral observer might have expected the French to win and go on to play the rather average Italian team in the final. Despite the French superiority, after two early goals, the score remained 1-1 for quite a long time. But then, in the twelfth minute of the second half, the German goalkeeper Schumacher made a scandalous foul on French player Battiston in the penalty area, knocking out two of his teeth and leaving the Frenchman unconscious for several minutes. Almost everyone in the stadium expected a penalty and a red card for the German, which would certainly have meant the Germans were losing the game. Indeed, this was the moment when the road to the World Cup opened up to the French, in a way visible to everyone. Only one person did not see it: the referee. He just gave the Germans a goal-kick, and the game went on without Schumacher being sent off. The score went to 3–3 in extra time, Germany won the penalty shoot-out, and Platini did not win the World Cup. At the decisive moment in his career there was neither fair play nor fairness.

Today, Platini is the president of the Union of European Football Associations (UEFA). Under his leadership, the organization has initiated a programme called Financial Fair Play (FFP). The programme has introduced rules for the financial conduct of clubs that play in European competitions. Roughly speaking, the basic rule is that every club should break even over a period of two or three seasons. In other words, the club's expenditures should not exceed its revenues over the period. When a club breaches the rule, it will be sanctioned. The strongest possible sanction is that the club is banned from European competitions.

The programme is making a gradual start. In the early stages, expenditures can still exceed revenues to a significant extent. For instance, clubs that had deficits of up to 45 million euros in total over the seasons 2011–12 and 2012–13 can still be in line with the regulations. Over the three seasons between 2014 and 2017, the sum total of a club's deficits can amount to 30 million euros. In the future, clubs will only be allowed to have, over each period of three seasons, a total deficit of 5 million euros at most. To keep the analysis simple, we can ignore these 5 million euros and simply say that clubs must break even in future.

UEFA hopes that its cooperation with national football associations will ultimately lead to a system where all clubs, including those that play in national competitions only, are strictly controlled. There are some hopeful signs. For instance, the clubs in the English Championship have already introduced their own version of FFP.

UEFA admits that its FFP system will probably turn out to have some shortcomings and that improvements will be needed. Thus, we will need to judge the system on how it works in the long run, when there has been sufficient time for improvements to take effect.

Taking this long-term perspective, the system will be critically analysed in a later section. But before we can do that, we need to discuss some other points. In order to make the discussion clear, it will be based on the following assumption: all professional clubs, including those at lower levels, will, from (say) 2018 onwards, be subject to an FFP system which works reasonably well to reduce the deficits. However, bear in mind that this is just an assumption; we will need to discuss whether it is realistic at a later stage.

One thing will not be discussed further, because it is not an assumption but something which is beyond any doubt; Michel Platini and the French team deserved to win the World Cup in 1982.

MORE MONEY THAN IS NEEDED

We have come to one of the central concepts of this book: economic rent. Here, we have to leave football for a while. We need to discuss some general ideas. It's going to be a bit difficult, but try to enjoy the game even so. Once you do, it will be easy going.

Put simply, there is economic rent in a particular sector of the economy if there is surplus money in that sector. To be more precise, economic rent exists in a sector when that sector fulfils the following condition: if the income of the sector falls (to a certain extent), it will nevertheless continue to produce the same amount of product, and of the same quality. Put differently, part of the money earned is not needed to keep production going.

Economic rent can have implications for economic policy. For instance, the government of a country could introduce high taxes in sectors that have economic rent. The companies concerned may not like it, but exactly because there is economic rent they will continue to produce goods. The tax revenues could then be used for schools, for instance. That would give more teachers a job. More importantly, it would increase production of goods and services in the future, when today's pupils start working. After all, the country's future firms will be better able to compete with foreign firms if their employees are well educated.

The revenues of high taxes in sectors with economic rent could also be used to reduce taxes elsewhere in the economy. Most sectors of the economy do not have economic rent. In these sectors taxes cause a reduction in economic activity, because they increase the costs of production. So reducing taxes in these sectors would boost production and employment.

In conclusion: when a sector with economic rent is taxed and the revenues are used to fund useful public projects such as schools, or to cut taxes elsewhere in the economy, this will lead to an increase in total production in the country.

To illustrate, let's use the classic textbook example of a tax on the possession of land by rich nineteenth-century landowners who are living in the city and renting out their land to farmers. The tax implies, obviously, that the landowners lose money. Of course, they would like to increase the rent they charge to farmers to compensate for this loss, but the situation is such that this makes no sense. The rents are very high already and at the limit of what farmers can afford. If they were increased any further the farmers would stop renting the land altogether and it would be left idle. So, since rents cannot be increased, the tax only leads to a reduction in the (net) income the landowners get from their land.

They continue to rent out the land to the farmers, because if they did not they would have no income from the land at all. The farmers are not affected and agricultural production remains the same. In this situation the income of the landowners is a form of economic rent; when it is reduced, economic activity remains the same.

Returning to the present day, the effects of taxation on economic activity differ from sector to sector. If, for example, a European country taxes the manufacturing of computers heavily, the manufacturers may stop producing in that country and move to Asia. This would be bad for domestic production and for employment. But if the country introduces a tax on land, the land cannot be moved to Asia and economic activities on the land may continue despite the tax. This could be a reason to make the tax on land higher than the tax on manufacturing computers.

It should be added that it is also possible that a high tax on land will cause production on the land to decrease. After all, at the present time, much of the land is owned by the farmers themselves and a tax may well reduce their budgets for investment. If agricultural production were to decrease, this would mean there would be no economic rent in the farming sector. However, in such a case, the following still holds: if the negative effect on economic activity of a tax on land were smaller than that of a tax on manufacturing computers, the former should be higher than the latter.

To be honest, I know little about the effects of a tax on land in the present day. The only reason for discussing this example is that it helps to explain three general rules of economics. These rules are as follows. First, to achieve high levels of production and employment, we should have high taxes in sectors with economic rent and lower taxes elsewhere. Second, when taxes lead to a small decrease in economic activity in some sectors and to a larger decrease in activity in other sectors, the tax rates should be higher in the former. Or, to put it more simply: taxes should be highest in those sectors where they harm activity the least.

Third, when the revenues of a tax are used for public projects which, taken by themselves, help increase domestic production, this will lead to an increase in production overall, as long as the tax itself does not reduce production too much. In this context it would be helpful if the tax were either a tax on economic rent, or a tax on sectors in which a tax does not cause too large a reduction in activity.

In the context of the story outlined above, an increase in production can be regarded as something that also leads to an increase in economic welfare. After all, economic welfare is the sum total of the well-being of all people in society, and an increase in production means that entrepreneurs and employees earn more money so that they can spend more on things which improve their well-being. So we can also say, for instance, that high taxes in sectors with economic rent can help improve economic welfare.

Finally, it should be emphasized that the argument is about economic welfare only, not about fairness. Thus, for instance, the question of whether landowners living in the city are lazy people deserving to be taxed is entirely irrelevant here.

A FOOTBALL TAX?

We can now discuss the possibility of introducing a special tax for professional football clubs at the European level. The tax is equal to, say, 10 per cent of the revenues of every club. So Manchester United will pay something like 45 million euros a year, and Ajax about 10 million euros. The 45 million from Manchester United will go to the government in London, and the 10 million from Ajax will go to the Dutch authorities. The only role of the European Union (EU) is to help ensure that all EU countries introduce the tax. In total, a 10 per cent tax for all European clubs will generate about two billion euros in tax revenues a year. This figure is based on the present levels of club revenues. Club revenues are expected to grow, which means the proceeds of the football tax are going to be higher still in the future.

What are the effects of the tax? Obviously, the authorities get a lot of money over the course of several years. Good! Think of all the school-children who will receive a better education if the billions are spent on that. Of course, the money could also be used in other ways. For instance, it could be used to reduce taxes in the manufacturing sector. The lower tax on manufacturing will then lead to more production and employment, because European firms will be able to compete better with Asian firms.

But what will happen in that poor football sector which has to take the full burden of the tax? Wrong question. The football sector is not poor. Let's try again. What will happen in the football sector?

Well, all clubs are confronted with the tax, and as a result their net revenues fall. To avoid losses they have to reduce their spending on players. The players will not stop playing, even though their salaries are slightly lower, and the quality of play will not be worse. In conclusion then, economic activity is not reduced and the football remains just as enjoyable as it used to be.

Of course, the tax will need to be announced well in advance so that clubs are given time to adjust their spending. Given the length of the existing player contracts, this could be done, say, five years in advance. After the five years, the introduction of the tax could be a gradual one. For instance, the rate could be set at 2 per cent first, at 4 per cent one year later, and so on. The FFP system will help club directors to reduce their spending to a sufficient level.

Some people will now remark that clubs in South America are not taxed, so that they can lure our top players away from us when player salaries are reduced in Europe. However, this danger is small. The largest South American clubs are far from being as rich as the largest European ones, and even with the tax they will not be able to hire top European players. Perhaps the tax will result in a few American talents staying one or two years longer on their own continent before moving to Europe, but this will not really harm the attractiveness of football in Europe.

So the tax will not have any serious negative effects on the football product offered. This implies that, basically, there is economic rent in the football sector. Indeed, the tax merely means that the clubs lose 10 per cent of their income, so that they are set back to the level of income they had just a few years ago. And at that time, they already proved that such a level is quite sufficient to produce high-quality play.

So we have concluded that there is economic rent in the professional football sector. This makes the sector a rather special one; most other sectors do not have economic rent. And so a tax on professional football clubs, the revenues of which are used to cut taxes in other sectors, or to finance useful public projects, will increase production and employment in the economy as a whole, and therefore improve economic welfare.

THE FEARS OF THE AJAX FAN

So far the football tax doesn't seem too bad. But the fans of Ajax Amsterdam may be getting a bit worried. They may be thinking: if the net revenues of Ajax decrease because of the tax, the club will have less money available for new players. This means it will be more difficult to sign up highly skilled, technical players, the type the club needs in order to live up to the high artistic standards of play set by Ajax in the past. Without players of this calibre, Ajax will no longer be able to distinguish itself from the other clubs – and it will be more difficult to beat eternal rivals Feyenoord. Indeed, with a football tax, the Sons of Gods, as the Ajax players are called in Amsterdam, will no longer play in heaven. Certainly, Ajax fans will not be happy.

This is a very interesting counter argument. However, the problem is that it is based heavily on the perspective of the individual club. In a way, this is to be expected. Ajax fans think a lot of their club, and when doing so they tend to ignore what happens elsewhere in the world. Indeed, they often seem to think that Ajax is the most important club in the universe. Outside Amsterdam, it is even said that Ajax fans are arrogant. That may be an exaggeration, but as an economist I have to teach the fans a lesson here: Ajax is no more than just one of the many football clubs. And when analysing the effects of a tax, you cannot neglect the other clubs.

Indeed, we should analyse the problem from the perspective of the football sector as a whole – and this changes the argument substantially. If all clubs are taxed, all clubs will have less money for players. As a result, player salaries will decrease overall and when all players are cheaper, it will also be possible for Ajax to buy good players – even though it has lower net revenues as a result of the tax.

So a football tax does not affect the quality of the play. The Sons of Gods will be as close to heaven, or as far away from it, as is normal.

WENGER AND MOURINHO

When it comes to a football tax, Arsenal fans may also have some doubts. They may think that when clubs earn less money they will also spend less on coaches, training facilities and youth development, with the result that the technical, tactical and physical capacities of the players will be lower, as well as the quality of play. Therefore, it seems that a tax reduces the quality of the football product so that there is no economic rent after all.

This seems to be a convincing argument. However, in an economic analysis it is not the quality of the players as measured along some objective yardstick that counts in the end. What really counts is the extent to which the fans are enjoying themselves, because this is what affects their well-being. It is true that Robin van Persie has great technical, tactical and physical capacity thanks to Feyenoord's youth development programme and Arsenal's excellent training staff. However, despite all such costly contributions to Van Persie's development as a player, he does not thrill the fans any more than George Best used to – even though Best's capacities may have been smaller when measured along an objective yardstick.

This is not to deny that, from the perspective of Arsenal, it makes sense to spend money on training players. After all, this can improve the quality of the Arsenal side. As a result, Arsenal fans will see their team win more often, which will certainly increase their well-being.

However, when viewed from the perspective of the football sector as a whole, the picture is different. As the technical, tactical and physical capacities of the players increase overall this will not lead to a proportional increase in the satisfaction of the fans. Admittedly, better training can lead to more skilled and beautiful play. Anyone who has seen the goals of Arsenal players Thierry Henry, Dennis Bergkamp and Robin van Persie, coached by Wenger, will agree with this.

However, better training can also improve the capacities of defenders, and of tough players who like to work hard, and this means there will be less room for attackers and for the creative, although possibly somewhat lazy, genius. No one who has seen Mourinho's Real Madrid crush the beautiful play of Barcelona can deny this fact. Therefore, increased investment in training overall will not improve the well-being of all football fans, or at best it will improve it by a small margin.

So we can still say there is economic rent in the football sector, or at least that there is a situation in which a reduction in revenues will have no more than a small effect on the quality of the product. This means that a football tax can help increase economic welfare because it will do little harm to football, while its revenues can generate large benefits elsewhere in society.

GEORGE BEST OR ROBIN VAN PERSIE?

Some people have a habit of paying a compliment before giving criticism, and so, some economists may say the following: that argument about the football tax was really very interesting from a theoretical perspective; however, there is no scientific evidence to support the part which concerns reality. There is no hard evidence that Robin van Persie does not give the fans more pleasure than George Best used to. More generally, there is no hard evidence that a football tax will not lead to changes in the level of play such that fans' pleasure is seriously reduced overall. And this means that there is no scientific proof that there is economic rent in the football sector.

This is entirely correct. But it does not mean we should not have a football tax.

Of course, we do not live in a theoretical world; we live in reality. But in reality policy decisions have to be made. One possible decision is to introduce a football tax and another one is not to. A choice has to be made.

To make a choice it is useful to get some answers to the following question: if we take a measure that results in spending less on players and their training, will this reduce the pleasure of the fans, and if so, to what extent? As there is no scientific evidence here, there is no alternative other than to base the answer on an assessment that is not scientific. The best thing is to make the assessment as good and as clear as possible.

Let me make my assessment clear. It is, to some extent, based on non-scientific sources, such as conversations with other football fans, articles written by sports journalists, and my own feelings as a fan. It can be expressed as follows. Reducing the salaries of the players by 10 per cent, or even more, will not make them play badly; the fans' pleasure will basically remain the same. And reducing expenditure on training will not make the sport much less enjoyable overall. Essentially, this means that there is economic rent in the football sector.

Many football fans may well have a different assessment here, and it may be better than mine. Some may think that high player salaries reduce the attractiveness of the game because, for example, players are spoiled by earning too much at too early an age. This implies that a football tax has an advantage which has been neglected by me: it helps reduce the bad influence of money on players. These fans may be right. However, this merely reinforces the conclusion that a football tax may be sensible.

Some other fans, however, may think that by spending large amounts of money on players and training the attractiveness of the game is increased considerably. Consequently, they may think that a football tax has a serious disadvantage which is ignored in this book. They may be right. How to weigh the disadvantage against the advantage of the football tax discussed earlier is up to them.

My assessment of the effects of reducing spending on players and training remains as stated above and, given that assessment, the remainder of the book will be based on the idea that there is economic rent in football. This implies that a football tax can improve economic welfare.

However, this does not mean that a football tax should be introduced. One reason is that the existence of economic rent also means that certain other policy measures may be useful for improving economic welfare, and perhaps even more useful than a football tax. Before making a choice, we should analyse all possible measures. The next section starts with the most obvious one.

ROYAL FEYENOORD

From 1995 to the present day, Dutch municipalities have spent hundreds of millions of euros to support their professional football clubs. Ajax, PSV Eindhoven, FC Twente – the list could go on – all of them have received tax money through investments in stadiums, lucrative land deals, loans or gifts. Over all these years, only one of the eighteen clubs in the Dutch top division of the 2013–14 season has not received any money this way: Feyenoord. Whatever cuts on schools and other useful projects the municipality of Rotterdam has made during these years, the club can take little of the blame.

In other countries there are many clubs that also receive large sums of money from the government. Taking Europe as a whole, we are talking billions of euros here. This leaves governments with much less money for other things. So the question is: is aid for professional football sensible?

In the foregoing sections, it has been argued that there is economic rent in professional football; the clubs earn more money than is needed to produce their matches. This means that they do not really need aid. It has also been argued that a tax on football clubs increases production and employment in the economy as a whole, and therefore improves economic welfare. Subsidies are the opposite of taxes, so it follows that subsidies for football clubs reduce production, employment and economic welfare. The reason is simple: with such subsidies, there is less money left for other useful purposes, and so all aid for professional clubs should come to an end. The government could use the money thus released to increase production, employment and economic welfare – through better education or lower payroll taxes, for example. Of course, when employment increases, unemployment goes down, so stopping the aid also reduces unemployment in the economy as a whole.

This argument can also be applied to subsidies for stadiums. In the distant past many clubs built a stadium without aid from taxpayers. Today clubs have much higher revenues, so all clubs should be able to build a stadium without aid. Neither is there any need to subsidize things such as youth development programmes. The football sector earns sufficient money to take care of that itself.

In reality, however, many football clubs do get support. Club directors defend this by saying that their clubs provide employment, generate tax revenues, contribute to social cohesion and do many other useful things. And one has to admit: football does make a valuable contribution to society.

However, it may come as a surprise to some club directors, but other firms also make valuable contributions to society. Every firm offers employment, and every benevolent firm generates tax revenues. In addition, pubs and nightclubs offer valuable contributions to social cohesion, while the same holds for the local company where people meet at the coffee machine. Indeed, the list of positive effects of firms is endless. And, believe it or not, there are also individuals who do useful things for society. If the government were to subsidize all firms and individuals that do such things, who would pay the taxes needed to finance all these subsidies? And who would pay the taxes needed to pay for the schools that educate the children who are going to make valuable contributions in the future? Indeed, there would be an unsolvable financial problem.

That's why, in the Netherlands, we have found another way to honour those who have made a valuable contribution to society: they receive a royal honour. Subsidies, on the other hand, should only be given to valuable activities that cannot be carried out without subsidies. In a sector with economic rent, such as the football sector, there are no valuable activities that cannot be carried out without subsidies, and the condition for giving subsidies is therefore not fulfilled.

In 1970 Feyenoord was both the first Dutch club to win the European Cup and the first to win the Intercontinental Cup. For many years the club has also been engaged in social projects. So surely the time has come for the King of the Netherlands to honour this great club with the highest possible award? Admittedly, Ajax, the club of the creative city of Amsterdam, has done some good things too. It has fielded creative players and demonstrated skilful play over the years. But Feyenoord, the club of the harbour-city of Rotterdam and of hard-working people, has taught the Dutch how to win. The club really deserves to be called Royal Feyenoord.

REAL MADRID, REALLY ROYAL?

In 2002 Feyenoord, the winner of the UEFA Cup, played Champions League winner Real Madrid for the European Super Cup. Feyenoord had a great team at the time. However, the year before Real had pocketed 480 million euros thanks to a land deal with Madrid's municipal council. This had enabled them to buy the world's best player at that time, Zinédine Zidane, for a record transfer fee of 77 million euros. Feyenoord lost.

The land deal was also noticed in Barcelona. One year before the deal, Barcelona's beloved star player, Luis Figo, had made a transfer to Real Madrid for a huge sum of money. Many Barcelona fans felt betrayed by Figo's move to the enemy. The Portuguese daily, *Diário de Notícias,* described the feelings of the fans by saying that Figo had represented the little that was left of the purity and romanticism in football, and that the transfer had turned him into the latest casualty of football's money grabbing. Apart from causing bad feeling, the transfer also contributed to Real's debt problem. And so, when this problem was solved through a land deal just a year after the Figo transfer, emotions ran high in Barcelona once again.

The question was asked as to whether the land deal was illegal in view of the rules of the EU for government aid. These rules apply to all organizations who are engaged in economic activities and sell their products on the market, including professional football clubs. Indeed, after some time, the European Commission started an investigation.

One of the principles of the EU is that all firms should compete on a level playing field. In other words, there should be fair competition. This principle has been given a prominent place in European law. As a result, governments are not normally allowed to support individual companies. The underlying idea is that, on a level playing field, only the better firms will survive and this will strengthen the economy.

Unfortunately, European law leaves much room for interpretation, and so when the European Commission has to apply the law to a concrete case it can face a difficult task. In the case of Real, the Commission started its investigation in a critical mood, suggesting that the price the club had received for the land may have been too high – which would have meant the deal was illegal. But in 2004 it closed the investigation, saying the price had been fair.

We cannot discuss all the legal details here, but one point is worth noting. One year before the land deal, the municipality of Madrid changed the legal status of the land, allowing the owner to turn it into a lucrative commercial zone after Real had moved its training facilities. This new land-use regulation immediately doubled the value of the land. So if, one year later, Real Madrid had not sold the land to the municipality but to private investors, the price would also have been higher, thanks to the change in land-use regulation.

So a major question is this: did this regulation represent a form of illegal aid? Here, EU law is ambiguous. According to legal scholars it can be interpreted in such a way that the regulation is illegal, but an opposite interpretation is also possible. However, if one goes for the first interpretation, a practical problem emerges. The regulation is one of the very many land-use regulations all over the EU, and such regulations affect all kinds of firms. Therefore, if the Commission had declared the regulation concerning Real's land illegal, it could have expected complaints about many other land-use regulations too. And so the EU could have become involved in all kinds of local and regional affairs. The decision on Real's land deal helped to avoid this. This may have been wise.

The lesson here is that there are always cases in which it is difficult to translate good principles into practice. If government support is based on land-use regulations, it may be especially difficult to prevent this sort of aid. But in many other cases government support consists of financial aid, by which we mean the use of tax money to finance gifts, loans and investments in stadiums or other club projects. Might it be easier to stop the aid here?

TOWARDS THE END OF FINANCIAL AID

So, we have this beautiful principle of EU law that all firms should compete on a level playing field. But once governments start to provide individual football clubs with money, some clubs will get more than others, so that fair competition is distorted. Therefore, it should come as no surprise that the European Commission has, in principle, a critical attitude towards financial aid for professional clubs.

For instance, in 2002 it explained in a letter to the Dutch government that financial aid for professional clubs was not allowed in a number of cases because it distorted competition. Among other things, it wrote that financial gifts were illegal. As a result, such gifts have completely disappeared in the Netherlands.

However, the letter from the European Commission was vague regarding some other forms of financial aid. This was related to the fact that the law allows exceptions to the rule. Of course, for an exception to be granted certain conditions have to be fulfilled. A crucial condition is that the aid helps realize social goals, and the Commission was of the opinion that support for football clubs can help realize social goals in some cases. Unfortunately, it did not fully clarify the legal implications of this opinion, and so the situation remained unclear.

In 2004, this prompted the Dutch government to write a report attempting to explain the Commission's letter to Dutch municipalities in order to help them avoid being sanctioned. The report said that, under certain conditions, the Commission allowed rescue aid, and aid for stadiums and youth development programmes, as such forms of aid could help realize social goals. However, some legal scholars did not agree and argued the Commission was more restrictive. So the legal situation has remained shrouded in mist.

Dutch practice since 2002 has been as follows: financial aid which is, in one way or another, related to the stadium, is frequently still provided. Rescue packages are also witnessed, often in the form of deals involving the stadium. Although on a few occasions the Commission has started an investigation to see whether a Dutch club has received illegal aid, sanctions have never followed. In other countries there has also been a large amount of aid which has not been prohibited.

The point remains that the football sector is earning economic rent. In principle it has sufficient money to take care of all its activities itself, including the activities that can help to realize social goals. For instance, the football sector can pay for its own stadiums and youth development programmes. Aid, therefore, is not necessary to allow clubs to realize social goals.

Admittedly, this only holds true in cases where the clubs are financially stable to begin with. For the time being, we are still assuming that UEFA's FFP system will work well in the future, leading to financial stability in the long term. We will see that this is a realistic view as long as the European Commission is willing to support UEFA in making the FFP system work well.

Of course, stability cannot be reached at short notice. In the next few years, some clubs may still need rescue aid to survive. Such aid will contribute to social goals because the continuing existence of a club normally brings benefits to society. And so rescue aid is, perhaps, legally justified in the short term. But in the long term, all clubs can be made financially stable, so that aid is no longer required. From this long-term perspective, all aid seems to be illegal; it makes the competition unfair, while it does not help realize social goals – since these goals can also be realized without the aid. And so, although I am not a legal expert, it seems to me that the Commission has a legal duty to stop all aid.

But even in the absence of such a legal obligation, the Commission has good reasons to stop all aid, with the exception of rescue aid, given in the next few years. Competition between football clubs should be fair, and it does not make sense to let taxpayers help finance stadiums and other club expenditures just to give clubs more room to offer their players ever higher salaries. It's time to stop this nonsense. It's time to act.

NO EXCEPTIONS, MR PLATINI

Until this point, the argument has been based on the assumption that, from (say) 2018 onwards, all professional clubs are subject to a FFP system, which works reasonably well to reduce their deficits. We can now discuss whether this assumption is realistic. Our starting point is the FFP system of UEFA, with the specific rules that UEFA intends to have in force after (about) 2018. We will discuss this system and its weak points, while also taking into account the possibilities for improvement.

The system's basic rule is that every club must break even over every three seasons. At least, this is how UEFA says the system will work. However, it should now be said that this is not entirely correct. Admittedly, the rule is that all expenses of a club should be covered by its revenues, but there are some exceptions.

Most importantly, the costs of investment in stadiums and youth development are exempt from FFP calculations. This is because UEFA and its chairman Michel Platini consider such investments to be valuable for the game and do not want them to be lower as a result of FFP. This sounds fine, but at the same time the revenues from these investments – additional ticket sales, for instance, or higher transfer fees – are taken into account when determining whether the break-even requirement has been fulfilled. What this amounts to is that clubs are allowed to make losses that are equal to their expenses on stadiums and youth development. And anyone who has some idea of the figures knows what this means: the losses, and the resulting debts, can be very large.

These exceptions also make it more difficult for UEFA to determine whether clubs are complying with the rules. To give one small example: the costs of cleaning the shirts of professional players count as expenses under FFP. The clubs, however, may put part of these costs in the books under the costs of cleaning the shirts of the youth players, that is, as costs of youth development, which do not count as costs under FFP. It will not be easy to detect such instances of foul play.

When clubs are making losses because of their spending on stadiums and youth development, who will pay for these losses? In countries like Spain, Italy and the Netherlands, this may well be the government again. The clubs will welcome such aid, of course. UEFA will also be happy with the aid, as the possibility of getting it will stimulate investments in stadiums and youth development. So UEFA may not want to make changes here.

This is where the EU comes in. It was argued earlier that the European Commission should try to stop all aid for professional football clubs, including the aid for stadiums and youth development. To this end, the Commission should ask, and if necessary force, UEFA to introduce a real break-even rule, so that investments in stadiums and youth development also count as costs. Of course, such costs can be spread over the years in the books, as is normal for investments. But the main principle remains: all costs are costs. This will make the FFP rules simpler and therefore easier to control. As a result, they will work better, and really prevent clubs from making losses.

This also implies that the curtain can fall on financial aid – as long as FFP encounters no other problems.

SIMPLY THE BEST

We have just seen that UEFA's FFP system could be improved if it dealt with costs in a better way. However, the system still has other weaknesses.

The first one is, in a way, related to men like Sheikh Mansour bin Zayed al Nahyan. Sheikh Mansour took over Manchester City in 2008. He spent a great deal of money on players, which brought the club the English title in 2012 and 2014. So the sheikh knows how to play the game. Other investors have also taken over clubs, with mixed results on the pitch. The financial results have also been mixed, with some clubs acquiring big debts. Later, I will give my own view on these developments. Here, the point is that UEFA wants to limit them.

Therefore, UEFA does not count injections of money coming from rich investors as revenues under FFP. This means that a club that receives such money and uses it to buy players will have higher costs in the FFP calculations but no higher revenues. This can cause it to be in breach of the break-even rule and be sanctioned.

Unfortunately, this rule causes problems. One well-known example concerns sponsorship deals. When sponsors pay a club to promote the name of their brand, the payments count as revenues under FFP and can be used to buy players. Donations of money coming from club owners, or from their friends and relatives, however, do not count as revenues under FFP and cannot be used for buying players. In the absence of any foul play, this limits the influence of big investors. However, some club owners may try to hide a donation behind a sponsorship deal, so that the donation looks like a payment for promoting a brand name, and then use the money to buy players. More generally, owners may find all kinds of ways to make capital injections count as revenues under FFP. UEFA will not always be able to detect such foul play, and this will reduce its credibility as a referee.

If such foul play turns out to be a serious problem, and if there are no effective measures to reduce it while still keeping the rules intact, it may be wise to stop using FFP to reduce the influence of rich investors altogether. All the money coming to a club could then be counted as revenues, which can be used to buy players; no exceptions. That would make control much easier.

If one still wanted to reduce the influence of rich investors, there may be other ways to do that. We will come to that later. For now the conclusion is that FFP may work best when it pursues one goal only: reducing the losses of football clubs. Simple play is often the best.

Another possible weakness of the FFP system is related to the fact that, to impose discipline on the clubs, harsh sanctions are needed now and then. It remains uncertain, however, whether UEFA is really capable of playing hard. UEFA is a union of national associations, and each national association holds power within it. And within the associations, the clubs hold sway. Partly as a result, the clubs have influence over UEFA. And the rich clubs have the most influence, as will be discussed in more detail later on. So if Barcelona is in full breach of the rules, will it really be banned from the Champions League? UEFA says it will, but will it live up to that ideal? If it does, UEFA is to be praised.

But in case it does not, it is good to know there is an organization that is still more powerful than the rich clubs: the EU. Its leaders, and the European Commission especially, have the power to ensure that punishments are sufficiently strong everywhere. But does the Commission want to help?

Earlier, it was argued that the Commission has good reasons for stopping all aid for professional football in the long term. This will increase production, employment and economic welfare. It will also make the competition fair. In relation to this last point, it was even argued that the Commission may well have a legal duty to stop the aid. However, these arguments were still based on the assumption that the clubs can be made financially stable. So the question left open is whether financial stability can indeed be reached. The answer to this question can be given now: yes it can, but only if the Commission supports FFP by assuring that sanctions are sufficiently strong (and by helping UEFA with other improvements).

And so, because the Commission has good reasons to stop all aid, it also has good reasons to support FFP. And, although I am not a legal expert, I can even say this: since aid makes competition unfair, the Commission seems to have a legal duty to support FFP. In any case, it is reasonable to expect the EU to help where necessary, and this will mean that harsh sanctions will be imposed and that FFP may work reasonably well.

If necessary, the engagement of the Union will also ensure that national football associations (helped by their national governments) use UEFA's FFP system, or a similar system, for clubs at lower levels. If that happens, financial control may work reasonably well everywhere. After all, the French experience discussed earlier has shown that, when the government is seriously involved and everyone keeps an eye open for possible improvements in the system, it is possible to impose financial discipline on football clubs.

So, if all necessary improvements are made, FFP will work reasonably well to reduce the deficits of all clubs. Perfection will never be reached, but the system will be simply the best.

BROTHER WALFRID AND A SOCIAL LEVY

In 1888, Celtic was founded by Brother Walfrid. He was a Catholic teacher who primarily wanted to use the club to help poor Irish immigrants. Part of the gate receipts went to the Poor Children's Dinner Table, which fed and clothed poor children. Initially, Celtic was above all a social movement, but precisely because of this it also grew as a football club. Before long, the club won the Scottish championship. Around the turn of the nineteenth century, with the help of thousands of volunteers, Celtic built what was then the biggest stadium in the world. And in the years before the First World War, the club played football at a level not previously seen. At that time there were no European cup competitions, but Celtic's tours attracted capacity crowds throughout Europe.

Celtic is still a socially minded club. But other clubs have shown that they can be socially minded too. English clubs have been strongly engaged in community activities for a long time. And the same thing is increasingly happening in continental Europe. Borussia Dortmund, for instance, strongly supports the fight against racism. And close to my home, FC Twente runs projects aimed at reducing school drop-out rates. Everywhere, there are success stories, in part thanks to the high profile of players among young people.

However, there are also many European clubs that do little in the social field. They prefer to use their money to strengthen their sides. This means that clubs that are socially active can only spend a limited amount on social projects, otherwise they would have too little left to invest in their teams – and these days that is a must for every professional club, because if the team plays poorly, results will suffer, leading to reduced revenues and perhaps relegation. In turn the club will become less popular and that will also affect its social projects. After all, the social projects depend on the standing of the players and the club.

Let me make a policy proposal. The EU, in consultation with UEFA, could demand that all clubs spend, say, 10 per cent of their team payroll – or in other words 10 per cent of their spending on players' wages – on social projects. The term 'social project' could be interpreted loosely. For example, supporting regional amateur clubs could be considered a social project. The clubs would be allowed to spend the money on social projects as they saw fit. We could call this measure a social levy.

For clubs that are already socially minded, such a levy might seem unnecessary, but in fact the reverse is true. Currently, if club A spends money on social projects while clubs B and C do not, this can adversely affect the quality of club A's side. This drawback will be removed if all clubs start investing in social projects.

The social levy will mean that all clubs will have less money left to spend on players. As a result, players' wages will go down across the board. The clubs will not go bust and will continue to produce high-quality football. Essentially, this is because there is economic rent. Therefore, a social levy may be a sensible measure.

Of course, the levy should be announced well in advance and the percentage of the levy could be 2 per cent at first, gradually rising to 10 per cent later. This would give the clubs the necessary time to adjust their spending, being helped by UEFA's FFP system where needed.

Earlier, it was suggested that it might be useful to introduce a football tax. However, making clubs pay both a tax and a social levy could be too much of the same thing. So it is sensible to make a choice.

In this context, the question arises as to which of the two alternatives is best for economic welfare. To find an answer, we need to compare the benefits of the social projects of football clubs with the benefits of using tax money for public projects (or the benefits of tax reductions). As yet, such comparisons have not been made and it will be difficult, if not impossible, to make reliable comparisons.

Still, a choice may need to be made in practice. To help us out, let's turn to the issue of fairness. Over the course of history many volunteers have contributed to the development of football, with the aim of increasing people's enjoyment of the game. The non-professional clubs, which have added a great deal to the game's popularity, are still social projects in this sense. A social levy would do justice to all those who have contributed to this social movement. And so my subjective choice would be to go for a social levy. I hope Brother Walfrid would approve.

A BAN ON PAY TV

What used to be free now comes with a price tag, and in the future the price of televised football may well increase further. In England, live Premier League games are only shown on pay TV. Plenty of people are prepared to pay handsomely to watch them, one reason being that only highlights are shown on free-to-view TV, usually late at night. In Italy, the situation is even worse. There, free-to-air broadcasters never transmit more than four minutes of Serie A highlights per day. Partly as a result of this, Italians pay a lot of money for extended highlights and live matches, which are broadcast on pay TV. In Spain, it's all about pay-per-view. It now costs more than ten euros just to watch Real Madrid–Barcelona on TV. And while all of this is going on, the politicians are enjoying their parties with the bosses of media companies.

In the Netherlands highlights of league matches are still free-to-air and can be watched at convenient times. Many other football matches are still broadcast for free too and, although some live matches are on pay TV these days, taken as a whole, watching football is still cheap in the Netherlands. Nevertheless, the Dutch do have a problem. Because foreign clubs earn a lot of money from selling their broadcasting rights to pay-TV channels, Dutch clubs are falling further behind financially. As a result they lose to foreign clubs more often.

What would happen if the EU introduced a ban on pay TV for all live matches and highlights shown in EU countries, so that they became free again? A ban would naturally mean that broadcasters would make less money. Therefore, they would pay the clubs less for their broadcasting rights. So the clubs would earn less and would have to moderate their expenditure. They could easily do this by paying the players less so that, on balance, they would not be disadvantaged. In the days before pay TV, clubs basically broke even, with lower income and lower expenditure and George Best producing beautiful play. So a pay-TV ban is perfectly possible. Indeed, the old economic rent argument applies: because there is economic rent a pay-TV ban will not harm the game.

Again, the ban would need to be announced well in advance, to give clubs time to adjust their spending patterns. An announcement five years ahead would be sensible. And all existing contracts between clubs and broadcasters could be respected. In some cases, this would mean that pay TV would exist for a little longer than five years.

But how would TV stations finance the broadcasts? That's simple: they would use the revenue from commercials. In the Netherlands, the highlights of matches in the second professional league have been broadcast free-to-air for many years by a private company. The league is not extremely popular, with an average match attendance of about 4,000. This means that advertising can generate sufficient revenue for broadcasting all football matches which are at least as important as those of the second Dutch level. So we would be able to have a pay-TV ban for all these broadcasts while being sure they will remain on the air. Additionally, this also means there is no need for broadcasters to use taxpayers' money to show football matches.

It was proposed earlier to stop government aid and to let clubs pay a social levy of 10 per cent. And now we are talking about a pay-TV ban. Are we harming the clubs too much? No. With all three measures in force, the clubs would still earn much more than they did twenty years ago, and their revenues will grow in the years ahead. Therefore, if all the measures are fully implemented in, say, ten years' time, the clubs' net revenues will probably be no lower than they are today.

So it is possible to have a pay-TV ban for all important football matches. Indeed, there is only one drawback: players (and coaches) would earn less. Whether this is fair or not is an issue for later.

The benefits of a pay-TV ban would be considerable. The first advantage concerns the football fans who would watch the broadcasts anyway: they would get them for free. Their savings would be more or less equal to what the players (and coaches) would lose through reduced salaries. If the savings for those fans were the only advantage of the ban, the question of whether we should have a ban would be a question of fairness only.

But the ban also has another advantage. This concerns football fans who do not watch (certain) football matches on pay TV because the subscription fee is simply too high for them. These fans will watch the broadcasts if they are free, because football gives them pleasure. For these people, a pay-TV ban would mean more pleasure. At the same time, the broadcasters' costs would not rise when more people turned on their television sets to watch football. So with a pay-TV ban we get more pleasure without any extra costs. This means that economic welfare improves.

In 1997, the EU took a remarkable step. It asked its member states to draw up a list of events that they wanted to be televised for free. A number of countries submitted a list. The Dutch one is strikingly long. As well as all kinds of non-footballing events, it included the highlights of matches in the highest Dutch league, European matches involving Dutch clubs, Holland's international fixtures, plus all matches at the final tournaments of the European Championships and the World Cup. This step may well be the main reason why so many football broadcasts are still free in the Netherlands.

Unfortunately, it also means that Dutch clubs earn less from pay TV than do foreign clubs. As a result, more players move abroad and the prospects of Dutch clubs in Europe decline. So the Netherlands may be tempted to cut down its list and other countries will be wary of adding to their own. For this reason the EU should become even more active.

The EU has often encouraged the free market, and this has been beneficial for many sectors. But the market does not always work well, particularly in football. In this case the EU needs to act by issuing a pay-TV ban for all important football matches. In this way it can demonstrate its social awareness, which is a necessity rather than a luxury if the EU wants to connect with the people.

NEW OWNERS

In 1983, Tottenham Hotspur was the first European football club to be listed on the stock market. In the next twenty years, dozens of other European clubs floated their shares. In 2003, the number of publicly traded clubs was close to forty. Since then it has decreased somewhat as a number of clubs have been de-listed.

Most clubs that were listed on the stock market were English. In legal terms being floated on the stock market was not such a big step for English clubs, because they had had shareholders since the start of the twentieth century. There was only one problem: around 1900 it had been determined that those shareholders could only receive limited dividends. By 1980, after many years of inflation, those dividends were worth practically nothing. However, this problem was circumvented with the help of some clever legal constructions, which effectively removed the limits on dividends. This meant that the shares in football clubs became more attractive for investors interested in profits and, as a result, clubs were listed on the stock market.

It is not true that all new owners were looking for profits; quite a few were still motivated by a desire to see the team win or to gain prestige. But some of the new shareholders were interested mainly in money. Until now, however, they have received a low return on average, so there will have been some disappointments.

Over the years, some of the new shareholders of the listed clubs acquired a majority interest and, with that, almost complete power over the club. In this way, these clubs started to resemble other clubs that had not been listed on the stock market, but had been bought by companies or individuals without going public. For instance, Paris Saint Germain became the property of media company Canal+ in 1991. This company sold the club in 2006 and, after being owned by other investors for a few years, the club is now the property of Qatar Sports Investments.

It can be noted that, despite all these developments, most professional clubs in continental Europe remain traditional not-for-profit organizations. Still, we should have a closer look at what the new owners have brought us.

Floating a club on the stock market, or selling it to a rich investor, leads to a short-term influx of money. The new money can be used to strengthen the side, among other things. An example is Chelsea, where the capital of Russian owner Abramovich helped the club win the Champions League in 2012. Many Chelsea fans will have been happy with Abramovich that year, and no one can blame them for enjoying their championship win and thinking of their club first.

But there is also another perspective; the one of all football fans when taken together. Each year, only one club can win the Champions

League. If Abramovich had not been on the scene, the fans of Bayern Munich, or Barcelona, might have celebrated their team winning the Champions League in 2012. So, on balance, Abramovich did not really have a positive effect on the well-being of all football fans taken together. Didier Drogba scored many wonderful goals in the Chelsea shirt, and two crucial ones during the 2012 Champions League final, but without Abramovich his goals might have brightened up the lives of the fans of another club.

The money of new owners has also been used to rescue clubs from bankruptcy. This may have been a good solution for some individual clubs, but from the perspective of football as a whole, it is doubtful whether being rescued by rich investors is necessary at all – especially in the future. If the FFP rules are strictly implemented, and improved where necessary, the number of clubs that need to be rescued from bankruptcy will be close to zero. And on the rare occasions that a popular club does go bankrupt, there will, in all likelihood, emerge a phoenix club, even in the absence of rich investors. After all, the administrator has to sell the club's assets to the highest bidder, and if a high bid from a rich investor is not forthcoming, he will have to accept a lower bid – for instance, from a supporters' trust that has gathered money from the fans. Indeed, in the absence of rich investors, the phoenix club of Glasgow Rangers would probably be owned by the fans now.

Some of the new owners have also used their money to build new stadiums. Good. But when FFP is in full force in the future, bringing financial stability to the clubs, no club will need a rich owner to build a stadium. After all, club revenues are many times higher than they were in the past, so that there is sufficient money to build beautiful stadiums anyway.

Although the money brought in by new investors can be beneficial for the individual club, there can also be a disadvantage at this level. Many investors take money out of the club sooner or later, through dividends or in other ways – at the cost of the club. The most extreme case is that of the 'leveraged buyout'. Here, the investor saddles the club with large debts in order to help finance his own purchase of the club. As a result, the club may lose a lot of money on interest payments and redemption, so that there will be less money for football purposes. So for some clubs, it is a significant problem that money can also flow in the direction of the owners.

As discussed above, there are also many cases where a new owner has brought benefits to a club. But, as also discussed above, these owners have not brought any substantial advantages to the football sector as a whole. Their large financial means seem impressive, but they do not mean much at all for the greater good of the game.

IN SEARCH OF A SOUL

In 2005, FC United of Manchester was founded by disappointed supporters of Manchester United. For quite some time, these supporters had been feeling that their old club was turning from a club with a soul into a soulless commercial enterprise. The takeover by the Glazer empire was the final straw, which led them to found a semi-professional club owned by the supporters only. The new club had to start at level ten of the English league system, but since then a few promotions have followed and FC United now plays at level seven, being watched by well over 1,500 spectators per match on average.

Supporters only leave a club they have loved – and they only invest time and money to create a substitute club that plays at a lower level

– when they are very dissatisfied with their first love. It is more than likely that there were many other fans of Manchester United who were also dissatisfied with the commercialization of their club but who did not sacrifice their relationship with their first love.

FC United is not alone. In modern times, England and Wales have witnessed the emergence of about a hundred supporters' trusts. Such a trust uses money obtained from a large number of supporters to acquire an equity stake in a club. Some trusts were founded with the immediate aim of rescuing the club, while other trusts started from the idea that supporters should have a say.

A number of professional clubs in the lower English leagues are now majority owned by supporters' trusts, one example being Portsmouth in League Two. Most trusts, however, have only a minority stake in the club. The trusts are especially important in the lower leagues. The only Premier League club in which a trust has a substantial stake is Swansea City, where the fans own seventeen per cent of the club. Minority stakes are used to influence club policies by, among other things, taking a seat on the board.

When members of supporters' trusts are asked to explain what the important things are about being a member, many of them say that they like to be represented as fans; to help improve the performance of their club; or to get a sense of belonging or solidarity. A survey among the fans of six supporter community-owned and five privately-owned professional football clubs showed that clubs owned by trusts gave more satisfaction to their fans than other clubs playing at the same level. From a scientific perspective, a caveat is in order here: these results cannot be taken as being representative of all fans of all clubs investigated; for some clubs the number of fans responding was too low to draw a reliable conclusion. However, the results suggest that leaving the ownership of a club fully in the hands of rich investors leads to reduced well-being of the fans. This means that there is a negative effect on economic welfare.

Combining this last conclusion with the conclusion of the previous section, which was that the new rich investors bring little benefits to the football sector as a whole (especially in the future), it follows that it is likely that the presence of these investors will, on balance, reduce economic welfare.

Therefore, policies that restrict the presence of such investors may be useful. Such policies do already exist. In Germany, for instance, there is a rule that private investors can own, at most, 49 per cent of the shares of a club. But overall, more could be done. For example, it may be useful to introduce the German rule in other countries, and perhaps the English government could back the supporters' trusts more, for instance through tax relief on their fundraising.

In the meantime, FC United is playing at level seven. There is an ideal, there have been promotions and there are high hopes. But some members may, just for a moment, be dreaming of those golden days of the past. They may think of Best and of Beckham, and of those two minutes in Barcelona when everything changed. They will see their old heroes sitting in Old Trafford, the theatre that still has top-level play. And for some of them, there may be some moments when it isn't easy to hold back the tears. But then, tears are forgiven as long as you fight.

PROFITS AND FAIRNESS

We can now turn to the issue of fairness, focusing first on profits. At the present time, most football clubs do not make significant profits. But some clubs, and especially the bigger ones, are gradually reaching a position in which they at least stand a chance to make large profits, and their chances may well increase in the future. One of the reasons is that Financial Fair Play may help them to limit players' wages. Other reasons will be discussed later on. But, whatever the reasons, new owners who have bought a bigger club with the aim of making large profits have a chance of reaching that goal, at least in the future.

Some of the policy measures discussed earlier can reduce such future profits. The two measures most likely to do this are the pay-TV ban and the social levy. The pay-TV ban reduces the revenues of the clubs, and the social levy obliges them to spend money on social projects. Therefore, these measures can, for clubs that make large profits, lead not only to lower players' wages but also to lower profits.

The question is whether such a reduction of future profits will be fair. Of course there can be no objective answer here. All I can do is give my argued opinion.

Let me first sketch out the broader context. Quite often it happens that a government pursues a policy which is meant to promote the common good, but which can be harmful for certain individuals or groups. And in some cases this has a big impact on those who are harmed. Just ask a 45-year-old government employee who has invested a lot in her job and is now losing it because of the government cut in expenditure with the aim of improving the country's future.

In most cases I agree with policies that promote the common good. But I also think there are a few cases in which the harm done to some groups is so serious that it can justify the decision not to pursue the policy. The final decision should depend on the case in hand.

The case in hand here is that of policy measures for football that improve economic welfare, which can be regarded as a common good. At the same time, they may harm the football entrepreneurs aiming to make profits. Taken on its own, this is a disadvantage. But is it sufficient reason for not introducing these measures?

I think it is fair that good entrepreneurs earn high profits. Take Steve Jobs. During his lifetime, his firm, Apple, brightened up the lives of people all over the world with many useful new products. Jobs earned a fortune with his work and in my opinion he deserved it, at least to a large extent.

But the new profit-seeking owners of football clubs have not made substantial contributions to the overall attractiveness of the game. Sure, some have made the fans of their team happy by luring good players away from other teams. But this has harmed the other teams. So, from the perspective of football as a whole, the contribution of the new owners is meagre at best. I wish them no ill. But if they were to make less profit in the future because of measures that promote the common good, this could not be a reason for not introducing these measures.

FAIR PAY FOR PLAYERS

Edson Arantes do Nascimento had the nickname 'O Rei do Futebol'. You know him as Pelé. He will forever be associated with that one display of skill at the 1970 World Cup in Mexico. From the halfway line, the Brazilian fired the ball over the Czech keeper, who was way off his line and turned to see the ball dip just in time. Nothing like it had ever been seen before during a World Cup match. Unfortunately, as a child in 1970, I was not allowed to watch it on TV because the match was broadcast late at night. So I was very pleased when footage from the game was recently broadcast on TV. And it was worth watching. The keeper was not even that far out of his goal – and the trajectory of the ball was even more impressive than I had imagined. Pelé even had a surprise in store for me: the ball went just wide.

These days you see the occasional lob like Pelé's – and now and then one goes in too. In 2014 Wayne Rooney scored a fantastic goal like that against West Ham United. Does that make him better than 'O Rei do Futebol'? Sadly, no. What made Pelé's lob so special was that he was the first who dared to try a lob in an important match. It may well be that the Pelé of old would have struggled in today's football. Today's players are physically and tactically stronger. No matter. Pelé gave people pleasure because he was better than his contemporaries.

What would have happened if the hundred best players of all time had never been born? Other players would have taken their places as superstars. Someone else would have been the first to lob the keeper from the halfway line. Of course, we would have had to do without a few delightful displays of skill, such as Maradona's sublime solo during the quarter-final of the 1986 World Cup in Mexico. Still, the pleasure had by all the fans put together would not have been much less as a result, because football's main attraction is the excitement and the contest against the opposition.

This brings us to the question of whether the present high player salaries are fair. In my opinion it is fair that a person's income is in line with what he produces at work, at least to a large extent. So what exactly is being produced by the top players?

Let's go back to that memorable quarter-final of the 1986 World Cup in Mexico, when Argentina played England. Some people think that Maradona scored two goals during this match, but according to the player himself one of the goals was made by the Hand of God. This goal is not the issue here; the question is not whether God is earning too much money, or whether his actions are fair.

The second goal from Maradona, the solo one, is the one that counts here. Many people regard this as the best goal of all time. Which factors determined the economic value of this fantastic goal? To begin with, millions of people watched the game all over the world. Taken by itself, this increased the goal's economic value. Indeed, this is simple: the larger the number of people who get pleasure from a goal, the higher its economic value. In 1970 television coverage was much lower than in 1986, and so, even if Pelé's 1970 lob had hit the net and had been regarded as the greatest goal of all time, the economic value of Maradona's goal would still have been larger.

Maradona scored some other magnificent goals during his career, but none of them was achieved in a match as important as a World Cup quarter-final. Indeed, it's not just the artistic value of a goal that thrills the fans. It's the fact that these artistic skills are exhibited in an important match, when tensions are high and nerves are fragile. Football is at its best when beauty arises in the middle of a mean and heavy fight, and Maradona had the talent to let beauty win this way.

Still, despite all his genius, he is not responsible for the fact that a quarter-final of the World Cup is an important fight. This is mainly due to the volunteers, supporters and rather poorly paid players of a previous era who made football such a popular sport. And above all, it's due to Nathaniel Creswick and William Prest, who founded the first football club and didn't ask for any money for doing so.

So the Maradona goal was great, but its economic value should not be exaggerated. If Maradona had not been there, somebody else might have made a decisive goal in the quarter-final of the World Cup played in Mexico City on 22 June 1986. Many would have enjoyed this other goal, although, of course, unless it were equal in artistry to Maradona's, total pleasure would have been much less because of the goal's lower artistic value. Now, the net contribution of Maradona's goal to economic welfare was equal to the value of his goal minus the value that the other goal would have had. And Maradona's reward for producing the goal should be equal to this difference – at least, if one is of the opinion that the salary of a person should be equal to the net economic value of what he produces.

The football clubs in the top divisions have very large revenues at present. They use part of it to pay for stadiums, electricity, cleaning services and other things that are necessary and cannot be obtained (much) more cheaply. If we subtract these unavoidable costs from the revenues, we get what could be called the 'net revenues' of the clubs. Details aside, nearly all these net revenues are used to pay players (and coaches). Put differently, the players (and coaches) get almost all the financial surplus. But their net economic value is much lower. This is because part of the surplus has been created by the volunteers and poorly paid players of the past, and by Nathaniel Creswick and William Prest.

So, in my opinion, the salaries of the present-day players are too high. It's not the stars who make football. It's football that makes the stars.

MONEY – A CURSE OR A BLESSING?

To summarize, there is more and more money in football, and this has changed the character of the game. Everything has become more businesslike. Supporters have to pay more to watch matches. The distance between clubs and their supporters has grown. Some clubs are owned by entrepreneurs in search of profits. And these trends seem set to continue into the future. Some see the money in the game today as a curse. They yearn for the past when 'everything was better'.

It is true that money brings dangers with it. But it offers opportunities too. We need to take advantage of the opportunities and avoid the dangers. Economic science provides a useful concept here: economic rent. Basically, economic rent exists in certain sectors of the economy, if the money earned in these sectors is surplus to what is necessary to produce the product. And in professional football there is economic rent. This offers the chance to improve economic welfare.

To begin with professional football is partly financed by the taxpayer, but, since there is economic rent, this is unnecessary and so the subsidies should end. After all, a sector with surplus money will continue to make a product even if the amount of money available decreases. The authorities could use the money so released in different ways, for example, by investing in children's education. That would lead to an improvement in economic welfare, particularly if today's pupils are better educated when they start work. But the money could also be used to help reduce payroll taxes, especially outside the football sector. This would also have positive effects on economic welfare.

A second possibility is to introduce a special tax for football clubs. The clubs may not like it, but, because economic rent exists, they will still continue to produce attractive football. The government can use the extra tax revenue to do useful things. However, this book is not really a call for higher taxes on football clubs. Instead, it is a call for a variation on higher taxes: a social levy, the proceeds of which are spent by the clubs on social projects. This will utilize the special qualities of football clubs in the social arena.

Third, we should have a European ban on pay TV, allowing all important football matches to be viewed free of charge. This means more people will get to enjoy football, leading to an improvement in economic welfare.

Finally, football does not really need the money of new investors. In relation to this it may be sensible to strive for an ownership structure in which the role of these investors is limited. This will make many fans feel more attached to their club.

All these measures will only make sense if the football sector is financially stable to begin with. At present it is not, as clubs are spending too much money on players. So before the measures can be introduced, there should be a robust system of financial control for all professional clubs. Such a system could resemble UEFA's FFP system, but it should also include a number of improvements, and the EU should support the system more actively.

All measures will have winners and losers. The winners may include: football fans, TV viewers, people who benefit from a football club's social projects and schoolchildren. The footballers will be the main losers in a financial sense, although top players will still get very rich. In the future especially, entrepreneurs aiming for profits through football may also be disadvantaged. Still, the measures will lead to an improvement in economic welfare. This means that the gain for the winners will be greater than the loss for the losers.

Even so, this is not enough for an economist to be able to conclude that the measures ought to be introduced. This is because science has little to say about whether the financial losses for players and club owners are acceptable. That is something everyone must decide for themselves. My opinion is that it is acceptable.

So my final conclusion is as follows. There is a lot of money in football these days. This offers fantastic opportunities to improve welfare. If we can make use of the chances, money will prove to be a great blessing.

3

DREAMS

THE MOST VALUABLE THINGS IN LIFE

It is said that the most valuable things in life are priceless. But what is the most valuable thing in life? It could be good health. Or love, or friendship. Or wisdom, as the Greek philosopher Socrates said. Whatever it is, many people think that the most valuable thing in life cannot be measured in terms of money.

Economists, however, sometimes try to express some highly valuable things in terms of money. For instance, they have estimated the value of a person's life. This may seem impossible, but if a man with two children dies because his workplace is unsafe and his wife wants compensation from the employer, her lawyer will need to express the value of the life lost in terms of money. An economist can be helpful in this situation.

Of course, it may not be wise to travel too far down this road. For instance, suppose you and your friend try to estimate the value you have on each other's well-being in terms of money, and your friend's estimated value is higher than yours. Would such a conclusion improve the friendship? Or is the basis of friendship that some things are not measured at all?

This being said, let us try to estimate the monetary value of professional football for the fans. Maybe we can learn something from this. After all, wisdom is one of the most valuable things in life.

The main value of professional football is that it provides pleasure for the fans. For convenience, the term 'fans' is interpreted broadly here; it means all people who enjoy watching football for a few minutes or more.

Consider a fan who pays 300 euros for a season ticket, and 200 euros for watching football on television over the season. This means his pleasure from football is worth at least 500 euros to him. But this is just a minimum. To get a better estimate, we could ask him what is the maximum amount of money he would be willing to pay for watching football, if the choice were between paying this maximum price or watching no football at all – not even on free-to-air television. Suppose he answers honestly that he is willing to pay 1500 euros per season. This means football has a value of 1500 euros for him, three times more than he actually pays. Now, if we ask all fans the same question and they all tell us honestly what football is worth to them, we can add up all the values given and get a figure that gives the total value of football for the fans, as expressed in terms of money.

Football also brings benefits to advertisers and sponsors, who pay clubs and broadcasters for this privilege. These benefits should be added to the value of football for the fans in order to get football's total economic value. Now, focusing on club football only, what would that total figure be?

Let us first look at what football fans, sponsors and advertisers pay for watching professional club football, or for getting other benefits from it. In the 2012–13 season they paid European clubs and broadcasters at least 20 billion euros. It could be a few billion more, but how much more exactly is not known. To be on the safe side, let's simply say the amount is about 20 billion euros.

However, it will be clear by now that the total economic value of professional club football may be much higher than the amount paid. Indeed, it could be very large. But how large?

In the example above we looked at a fan who paid 500 euros a year for watching football, while valuing football at three times that amount. Let us look at some other examples now. First, consider a fan who pays 180 euros a year for football and cannot afford to pay one cent more. So if we ask him what the maximum amount he is willing to pay is, he will say 180 euros. Therefore, for him the value of football is just 180 euros. Indeed, this is how economists think: if a person has a small budget, then for him the value of football as measured in terms of money cannot be high – however much he may love the game. Next, consider a dedicated Juventus fan who pays 4000 euros and who is a billionaire. He may be willing to pay 80,000 euros if necessary, twenty times more than he actually pays. Finally, consider an 85-year old Dutchman who watches many important football matches free of charge on television. He would be willing to pay 300 euros for this at most, if he had to. So football is worth 300 euros to him, while he actually pays nothing at all.

These examples suggest that it is not impossible that the value of football for all fans put together is, for instance, four times higher than what is actually paid. At the same time, it will also be clear that any estimate of this value is pure speculation. Regarding advertisers and sponsors, I make just one remark: a number of them may, if necessary, also be willing to pay more than what they actually pay, but the difference may be relatively small in this case.

So the amount actually paid for football is about 20 billion euros, while the value of football is higher. It may be worth something like 60 billion euros a season, or even more. This is not impossible, but it remains speculation. After all, the most valuable things in life are priceless.

WHAT SHOULD COUNT MOST?

The economic value of European professional club football may be some 60 million euros a year. This figure represents the benefits of this part of the game. But to get the net contribution of (this part of) football to economic welfare, or in other words, football's net economic value, we should also take the costs into account. More precisely, we should subtract the costs from the benefits. So, what are the costs?

For the 2012–13 season the financial costs of the European professional clubs, plus the financial costs incurred by broadcasters for filming their matches and adding comments and other content, can be estimated to be somewhere around 20 billion euros (which happens to be close to the financial revenues). This figure for financial costs may be regarded as a reasonable estimate of the costs of football for society. It can be noted here that some economists may argue that the true costs of football for society are lower than its financial costs, but to keep the story simple we will ignore this view – also because it does not really change the main conclusion outlined below. So let us simply say that the costs are about 20 billion euros.

If the benefits of professional club football are around 60 billion euros, and the cost about 20 billion euros, then football's net contribution to economic welfare will be something like 40 billion euros. Of course, we could have a longer discussion about this estimate. Maybe it should be 30 billion instead of 40, or 60 billion perhaps? But in all likelihood, the main conclusion would be this: professional club football's net economic value is in the order of tens of billions of euros. That doesn't seem bad. I wonder whether football's founding fathers could ever have dreamed of that.

Perhaps you think these are just some funny facts – to be talked about in the pub. But this is a serious book. And the fact that the benefits of club football for society are so much greater than the costs has an important policy implication: in order to improve economic welfare it is very important to increase the benefits.

Essentially, this means it is crucial to increase the pleasure of the fans. This will be good not only for the fans but also for advertisers and sponsors. After all, their commercial benefit from football depends strongly on the number of people watching and, therefore, on the attractiveness of the game to the fans. So fans' preferences should count the most. Of course, one should never forget the financial costs as they can cause serious problems for the clubs. But as argued previously, with FFP in full force, it should be possible to avoid such problems.

With this in mind, the remainder of the book will focus on the benefits of football and on how the wishes of the fans can best be satisfied. From now on it's all about the attractiveness of the game.

There are many different factors that affect the attractiveness of football matches. Some of these factors are taken care of at individual club level, such as the design of the stadium, the style of play and how the club is positioned in the community. Architects, coaches, club directors and other people know much more about such things than I, and it would be useless to discuss them here.

There are also factors beyond the level of the individual clubs that affect the pleasure of the fans. Most of the remainder of the book will focus on two very important ones: the differences in playing strength between the teams and the structure of the competitions. Here, improvements always require cooperation between clubs and possibly even government intervention.

But all this is for later. First, we need a broader and inspired view. At this special moment, it is my great honour and pleasure to introduce a brilliant entrepreneur and a real sports fan. A man with a vision. Please give him a warm welcome.

BILL VEECK

Bill Veeck served in the United States Marine Corps during the Second World War. He returned home after being injured and, after many operations, lost much of his right leg. But he was an optimist and wanted to keep life as enjoyable as possible. So he had an ashtray built into his wooden leg. And, being a sociable smoker, he liked to use it.

He was also a businessman. After the war, he was at various times the owner of three different Major League Baseball clubs: the Cleveland Indians, the St Louis Browns and the Chicago White Sox. He became a prominent figure within the sport. In America he was said to be the greatest promoter of professional team sports ever. With his creative mind, he brought many new elements to the game. In 1960, as the owner of the White Sox, he introduced the exploding scoreboard. It produced fantastic sound effects, and fireworks exploded whenever the White Sox hit a home run. He was also the first to put players' surnames on the back of their uniforms, and he had many other good ideas. Behind all these things was the business instinct of Bill Veeck, and his entrepreneurial vision was actually really simple: professional sports clubs are selling dreams.

It is difficult to trace the way in which ideas spread over the world and we will never know precisely to what extent Veeck's vision inspired European clubs. However, the fact is that European footballers started having surnames on the back of their jerseys long after Veeck introduced this practice in American baseball, and Veeck presented his vision of sports and dreams long before Old Trafford got its nickname, 'The Theatre of Dreams'.

Earlier, a distinction was made between the concept of economic welfare and that of fairness. Economic welfare is the sum total of the well-being of all people as expressed in terms of money. We have seen that questions about this sum total can, in principle, be answered in a scientific way. But whether things are fair is a question which can only be answered subjectively.

Because the concepts of economic welfare and fairness are so different, economists often neglect the relationship between them. However, being inspired by Bill Veeck, we should now discuss whether feelings of fairness can affect economic welfare.

Fairness has an effect on economic welfare whenever fans' feelings of fairness affect the pleasure they get from the game. For instance, when some football fans feel it is unfair that the money of billionaires determines who is able to win the people's game, such feelings are part of reality. Moreover, when such feelings reduce the pleasure of these fans, or even causes some of them to turn their backs on football, their well-being decreases – which means economic welfare decreases. Indeed, in terms of economic welfare there is no distinction between people who do not like football for 'objective' reasons, such as having to sit in the cold, or people who do not like it for 'subjective' reasons, such as a dislike for big money. The only thing that counts is the total amount of pleasure of the fans, whatever the reasons.

When a person prefers watching baseball to watching football there is no objective reason for that. And whatever it is that makes people like Ajax, it must be based on emotions. Of course, many people like to sit in comfortable seats, and this is rational. But more importantly, in the theatre of dreams you want to have pleasant dreams, so whenever your dreams are tossed and blown about by unfair things, economic welfare decreases. That's a hard fact.

GRANDSTAND MANAGERS DAY

After the St Louis Browns had lost four times in a row, its owner, Bill Veeck, found some new inspiration. On 24 August 1951, when the Browns had to play a home game against the Philadelphia Athletics, he organized 'Grandstand Managers Day'. To assist the home team, the 1,115 fans who had tickets to a seat behind the dugout were given the chance to vote on in-game strategic decisions. The first vote came immediately during the first inning. The Athletics had taken a 3–0 lead, with one out and men on the corners. The question was whether the infield of the Browns should remain positioned at double-play depth. A sign was held up above the dugout, asking the 1,115 managers what to do. They could show a white card for 'yes' and a red card for 'no'. The majority showed white. That appeared to be the correct decision, and quickly led to two runners heading out at the same time. In the meantime, coach Taylor comfortably smoked his pipe in a rocking chair next to the field. It was hot, but he had cool drinks within reach. It became a gruelling match and the public had to take some pretty hard decisions. One of them was completely wrong, but most were decent decisions. In the end, the Browns won 5–3. Grandstand Managers Day was simply great.

Despite its success, the experiment was not repeated, and, apart from the exception that confirms the rule, there may be good reasons for letting in-game strategic decisions be taken by a manager who is working with the team on a daily basis.

Elsewhere in society, however, decisions, in quite a number of cases, are taken on the basis of a vote. Most countries are democracies in which citizens vote about the general direction the country should take and decide who will take responsibility for more specific problems. Some countries also have referendums about specific issues. In Switzerland, for instance, many decisions are taken by referendum each year. To give just one example: in 2008, Swiss voters decided on a package of measures in the field of soft drugs.

Many of the following sections will focus on specific policy measures and their pros and cons. For every measure, the main question is whether it can help improve economic welfare. In answering this question, it will always be kept in mind that to improve welfare, the wishes of the fans should be satisfied as much as possible.

Unfortunately, it will not always be possible to get reliable scientific answers; sometimes, scientific evidence on the preferences of the fans is hard to obtain, and so we might take some comfort in the idea that it might one day be possible to have a vote in which all football fans, or at least all football fans who are members of an official supporters organization, are asked which measures should be introduced to improve the people's game. Wouldn't we all then play a part in the real theatre of dreams?

4

NO EQUAL CHANCES

MORE CHANCES FOR THE BIG

At the present time, a small number of clubs have come to dominate the football competitions. In the ten seasons from 2004 to 2014, only seven different clubs reached an end-of-season top-four position in the highest English league at least once. In the ten seasons from 1960 to 1970, there were fourteen different clubs that managed this, including clubs like Sheffield Wednesday, Derby County, Leicester City and Ipswich Town. In those days it was good to live in a town like Ipswich and watch your local club.

From 2004 to 2014, only fifteen different clubs reached the semi-finals of the Champions League. From 1960 to 1970, there were twenty-five different clubs that reached the semi-finals of the European Cup. Here, the situation has deteriorated, especially for clubs from the smaller football countries. From 1960 to 1970 a club from a country outside England, Germany, Spain, Italy and France reached the semi-finals of the highest European tournament sixteen times. Since the summer of 2004, such a thing has happened only once – in 2005, with PSV Eindhoven.

For the Netherlands, the story is a particularly sad one. Dutch clubs have won the highest European title six times in total between 1970 and 1995, but many people now think that a Dutch club will never win it again. Portugal, Scotland, Romania and Serbia also have clubs that have won the highest European title in the past, while clubs from countries of this size have negligible chances at present.

Of course, one should be careful with occasional statistics such as the ones above, so let us see what economic science has to say on the issue. First of all, we need to be clear on terminology. Competitive inequality, or competitive imbalance, means (as you may have guessed) that there are differences in the playing strengths of the teams participating in a match or competition. As a result, some teams have a greater chance of winning than others. Uncertainty of outcome means that the outcome of a match or competition is difficult to predict. Predicting the winner is most difficult when the teams have almost equal playing strengths. And when competitive inequality is increased, uncertainty of outcome is decreased.

Economists have analysed uncertainty of outcome from different angles. Some have investigated whether the uncertainty about the results of individual matches has decreased over the years. Others have focused on the predictability of the outcome for the season. Here, one of the questions is whether it is always the same teams that win the title over the course of the years.

The results of the scientific investigations do not always point in the same direction, but the majority of the evidence suggests that uncertainty of outcome has decreased over the years, especially if one looks at a long period of time – say thirty years or more. Put differently, competitive imbalance has increased over the long term. But there are exceptions. For instance, in the Spanish league Real Madrid and Barcelona do not seem to be any more dominant than they were fifty years ago.

In view of the majority of the evidence, the analysis below will be based on the idea that, exceptions apart, there is a long-term trend towards increasing competitive inequality.

How do differences in playing strength come into existence? They are caused to a large extent by the disparities in income among the clubs. In recent times, the richer clubs in particular earn ever more money, most of which is used to buy players. As a result, most of the better players go to the big clubs at an ever younger age, although some of them sit mainly on the bench when they get there.

This process has a tendency to reinforce itself because of the way the market works. Clubs with a lot of fans have big revenues as a result. Therefore, they are able to buy good players and win more often. Due to their successes on the pitch they get even more fans, generating still more income and the ability to buy even more good players. In this way, inequalities continue to rise.

Of course, such mechanisms existed in the past too but the effects were more moderate then. In past times revenue came mainly from gate receipts. The size of a stadium has always been subject to physical limits. In addition, supporters prefer not to travel too far to watch a match. For this reason, the revenues that Real Madrid derived half a century ago from winning the European Cup five times in a row were substantial, but still remained within bounds. At that time, Scotland's Celtic, with a stadium not much smaller than the Bernabéu, had revenues not much below those of the Madrid club. Against that background, it was still able to make a difference with regional talents, a tough mentality and an excellent coach. This enabled the club to win the European Cup in 1967. Indeed, for the clubs from smaller countries such as Scotland, those were the golden days in which vision, talent and mentality were more important than money.

Currently, revenue is mainly determined by the number of television viewers, which is not bound by physical limits. As a result, success on the field now impacts more on income. As in the past, Real Madrid wins major honours. But these days, those honours mean the team appears on TV with greater frequency in Spain and elsewhere in the world. This ensures that the club earns huge amounts of money from its broadcasting rights. Thanks to television, Real even attracts fans from Asia. That in turn boosts sponsorship revenues and sales of club merchandising. However, clubs that play fewer big games, such as Celtic, Rangers, Aston Villa, Benfica, Anderlecht, IFK Göteborg, Saint-Étienne and Panathinaikos, are falling further and further behind when it comes to TV-related income. In this way, the market mechanism is resulting in ever greater imbalances on the field.

But is this a problem? Should football be a socialist game?

DAVID AND GOLIATH

We have come to the subject of the impact of competitive inequality on economic welfare. As noted before, economic welfare is the sum total of the well-being of all people in society, so the welfare generated by football essentially depends on the sum total of the pleasure of all football fans.

Let us start with a simple question: would the fans have much pleasure if there were no inequalities at all? This is an unrealistic case, of course, but economists like such cases because they can yield useful insights. So, in this case, the twenty Premier League clubs all have equal playing strengths. In August, bookmakers give both Liverpool and Swansea a five per cent chance of winning the title. Both clubs can expect to become champions once every twenty years. Or, to be precise, less often than that, because there will always be clubs that get promoted to the Premier League, resulting in more than twenty clubs having a chance of winning the English title one day.

This all sounds reasonable but there is a problem. Swansea has relatively few supporters, so when it wins the title the number of people celebrating the victory will be limited. Liverpool has many more supporters so a Liverpool win will improve the well-being of many more faithful club fans. So, if we want economic welfare to be high, Liverpool should win the title more often than Swansea – simply because more people will then have pleasure. For economists, numbers count.

Does this mean that welfare will be highest when the club with the largest number of fans, Manchester United, wins the English title every year? No, because in this case there is no surprise. Even if United loses a match here and there, this will be no big issue because the club will finish first anyway. United fans will get bored, because they are certain to win the title year after year. Fans of other clubs, who know their club will never win the title, will no longer find the sport really entertaining. And the neutral football fans will become indifferent towards football. After all, if the question of who wins becomes unimportant, football has little to offer.

In present-day reality, Manchester United wins many English titles but is far from winning them all. Still, the pleasure which a United fan gets from a new title is, on average, much smaller than the pleasure of a fan of a club that wins the title for the first time in more than forty years – as those who saw the fans of Manchester City celebrate their 2012 title will readily confirm. So perhaps we should hope that the next five seasons will be as bad for United as 2013–14, so that its fans will have an extraordinary feeling of happiness should the club regain the title in 2020.

Furthermore, if Swansea were to win the title next year, the pleasure of the average fan of the league champion would possibly reach an all-time high. In addition, people who have sympathy for the underdog would also be pleased. A Swansea title would show that, however hopeless a situation may seem, and however life turns against you, hope is always justified. This will also make the fans of other clubs feel better during the next season, since much of their pleasure is based on hopes and expectations. Indeed, this is what Bill Veeck taught us long ago: sports clubs produce dreams. And to enable fans to dream, it would help if clubs like Swansea had some chance of winning the title one day in the future.

Some economists advocate large competitive imbalances by referring to the story of David and Goliath. This story, they say, is so popular exactly because David was so much weaker than Goliath. They have a point. God knew what he was doing when he let David fight a giant and gave him a very small chance of winning. After all, if David had had zero chance, there would have been no story at all. Like so many stories, the story of David and Goliath has two sides.

Today, the chance that Swansea will win the Champions League is basically zero. And worse, the same holds for Celtic and Feyenoord. Of course, we should always have our dreams. But sometimes it's difficult to walk on with hope in your heart.

LIES, DAMNED LIES OR GOOD STATISTICS?

We have seen that full competitive equality does not promote economic welfare, whilst it is also undesirable that competitive imbalances are too large. We need to be somewhere in the middle. But where exactly? Perhaps statistics can help here. Statistics can be difficult, but let us start with some simple facts.

In the twenty seasons between 1991 and 2011, competitive imbalances in the highest English football league (named the Premier League since 1992) increased. At the end of this twenty-year period the stronger teams were able to win still more matches than at the beginning of the period and the teams ranked lowest had even fewer points in the final ranking. You may have noticed this trend yourself, but I would like to add that this trend is confirmed by reliable statistical research.

During the 1991–92 season, the clubs in the highest league pulled in 10 million spectators. In the 2010–11 season, they had 13.4 million visitors. So over twenty years, attendance grew by 34 per cent, despite a large increase in ticket prices. Clearly, the top league had become more popular.

So during the twenty years from 1991 to 2011 more people came to watch, while competitive inequality increased. Doesn't this show that more inequality makes the game more attractive?

No. Such a conclusion would be much too simple. There are many other factors that affect the popularity of the game. During the same twenty seasons, the English stadiums became more comfortable and the problem of hooliganism was successfully tackled. In addition, many of the world's top players came to play in England and the quality of play, when compared to other countries, improved markedly. All these factors helped to make the English top league more attractive. And you can probably find some other factors that have made it more popular since 1991. Now, it is possible in principle that the increase in spectators between 1991 and 2011 was caused entirely by the factors just mentioned, and not by the increase in competitive inequality. Therefore it cannot be concluded from the figures above that more inequality makes the game more attractive.

If you like simple facts, I'll give you some more. What do you want? Facts which suggest competitive imbalance is bad? As you wish. In the 1949–50 season the English top league pulled in 17.4 million spectators. In 2010–11 it had only 13.4 million visitors. In 1950 there was much more competitive balance than in 2011; many more teams had a chance of winning the title. These facts may suggest, at first sight, that the increase in competitive imbalance which has occurred between 1950 and 2011 has caused attendance to drop. But in fact, such a conclusion makes no sense. There are so many other factors that may have caused the decrease in attendance.

There can be only one valid conclusion: we should be careful when drawing conclusions here.

Good statisticians are no liars. They produce reliable and useful results. They use the best available methods at the time. Unfortunately, these methods cannot lead to reliable results in all cases. The chance of being wrong depends on the subject, and the effect of competitive inequality on the pleasure of football fans is a difficult subject. This does not mean it is impossible to get good results, but it's an uphill struggle.

Over the past years, a number of studies on the effects of competitive inequality in European football have been carried out. There is neither the time nor the space to discuss all the studies here, but it can be said that there are different and sometimes opposing results. Many statisticians see this as a challenge. That's good, but in the meantime, we do have a practical problem: if we do not know whether the present imbalances are too large or too small, how do we know whether we should have more or fewer policy measures for reducing competitive imbalance?

MAKING A CHOICE

In practice, choices have to be made. One choice we can make now is to reduce competitive inequality (if this is possible). Another possible option is to increase it. A third option is to leave things as they are. Indeed, doing nothing is also making a choice. One way or the other, a choice has to be made.

What advice can I give here? I can give 'my view as an informed economist'. That view is that we should try to decrease competitive inequality. But what does this 'view as an informed economist' mean? It is a view based on scientific arguments. These arguments are given in the online supplement to this book. In this, the studies of other economists are discussed. Some economists advocate one view, while others lean towards the contrary. All in all, economic science can offer no certainty at present, but I can present my own arguments. Taking account of the results from the other studies, I conclude in the supplement as follows: it is plausible that the level of competitive inequality has become too high at present, or will become so in the near future; therefore we should try to reduce it.

If you read the supplement, or, even better, if you also read the works of other economists, you can make a judgement yourself. But if you do not have time for this, please be aware of the uncertainties surrounding my advice.

I should also add something else here. In principle, we could have started out from a totally different perspective: suppose all football fans could vote on the issue, and suppose that the majority voted for reducing competitive imbalance. Would that mean that the imbalances are larger than is good for economic welfare? There is a big chance they would be. After all, economic welfare is the sum total of the well-being of all individuals. And to improve economic welfare in football the main thing is to let the fans have more fun. So if the majority of fans vote to reduce imbalances it is likely that this will indeed improve economic welfare.

However, the outcome of a vote amongst the fans will not always tell us what is best. Fans can also make all kinds of mistakes. For instance, some fans buy a season ticket and realize after four matches that showing up every two weeks is too much for them. So when a fan thinks that more competitive balance will give him more pleasure in the future, he may be wrong.

And there is another problem. Suppose that 60 per cent of the fans vote in favour of reducing competitive imbalance, while 40 per cent vote against. Suppose also that most of those in favour are just occasional television viewers, while most of those against are diehard fans. In that case, it is still possible that the sum total of the well-being of all fans will be highest if imbalances are not reduced. This example shows that majority voting can lead to lower economic welfare in some cases.

In most cases, however, the vote of the majority will probably give the correct answer to the question of what is best for economic welfare. In addition, the following may hold: if fans have more influence, then, whatever the decisions they help to take, they will derive more pleasure from the game because they can regard it as their own. A real 'people's game', as it were. So it may well be best to follow the vote of the majority instead of the advice coming from an 'informed economist' who emphasizes there are many uncertainties surrounding his advice.

The Football Supporters' Federation is a democratic organization which represents more than 500,000 football fans from England and Wales. The Federation is of the opinion that there is too much competitive imbalance at the present time. It is not unlikely that this reflects the opinion of the majority of its members. If this were indeed the case, and if the majority of the football fans outside the federation thought the same way, then, according to the majority of the fans, the level of competitive inequality is too high.

Unfortunately, we do not yet have all the information that is needed to draw such a conclusion. But perhaps, one day, we could have a kind of referendum among well-informed football fans to see whether most of them think that competitive inequality should be reduced. What would Bill Veeck have thought of that?

Whatever the merits of voting, the remainder of this book will be based on my view as an informed economist, and that view is that competitive inequalities should be reduced. But this immediately leads to another question: how can we do that?

SIMPLE PLAY IS THE MOST DIFFICULT

Former Barcelona coach Johan Cruijff is known, amongst other things, for his philosophical insights. A typical quote of his is: 'Simple play is also the most beautiful. How often do you see a pass of forty metres when twenty metres is enough? Or a one-two in the penalty area when there are seven people around you and a simple wide pass around the seven would be a solution? The solution that seems the simplest often is the most difficult one.'

If we want to reduce competitive inequality, let us look for a simple method first. We have seen that an important reason for the increase in competitive inequality is the rise in TV income, from which the big clubs in particular benefit. Therefore, to reduce the inequality it may make sense to diminish the weight of this source of revenue. A way to achieve this would be a ban on pay TV for all important football matches. Pay TV would then generate practically nothing, so that TV income would fall.

We have talked about this pay-TV ban earlier in the book. There, we were discussing pay TV in isolation, removed from the problem of competitive inequality. It was argued that pay TV reduces the number of viewers and therefore the pleasure from football overall. A pay-TV ban would increase the number of viewers again and therefore improve economic welfare.

However, we now run into another aspect of a pay-TV ban: it would reduce competitive inequality. How would it do this, exactly? The ban would cause TV income to fall. As a result, the share of revenues related to stadium visitors, including gate receipts, as a proportion of total income would rise. Such revenues tend to be divided more equally between the clubs than TV income. The loss of the income from pay TV would therefore mean that total revenues would end up being more evenly divided between the clubs. This would reduce competitive imbalances on the pitch. It's a simple method. And if something is simple, why make it difficult?

Unfortunately, a pay-TV ban would only reduce the imbalances to a limited extent. The main reason is that much of clubs' TV-related income is unconnected with pay TV, and this income would therefore not be affected by a pay-TV ban. The income referred to consists of revenues from commercials shown around televised football (which largely go to the clubs in the end), revenues from shirt sponsorship and revenues from the sale of club merchandise. Such revenues depend to a large extent on the number of television viewers, and they are distributed very unevenly between the clubs.

In addition, even without television, there would be some serious competitive imbalances. This is because receipts related to stadium visitors are unevenly distributed too, albeit to a lesser degree than TV-related revenues.

Indeed, the football sector recognized the problem of competitive imbalance long ago. Even in the time before television, when the problem was less pronounced, measures were introduced to make the sport more competitive. For instance, in the nineteenth century a transfer system was introduced. What happened to the measures introduced in the past and do they still exist?

THE TRANSFER SYSTEM

Jean-Marc Bosman was a player with Belgian club RC Liège. In 1990 his contract expired and he wanted to move to the French club Dunkerque. However, he was unable to do so because Liège demanded too high a transfer fee. Bosman took his club to court. The case eventually went to the European Court of Justice, the highest court of the EU. Bosman invoked the principle of free movement of workers, which had been part of European law since 1957. In 1995, after five years of legal struggle, the Court vindicated Bosman: it ruled that players whose contracts had expired could move clubs on free transfers. This ruling will remain in force as long as European law is not amended.

The ruling has not only affected out-of-contract players; it has also had a moderating effect on the transfer sums paid for players with ongoing contracts. The reason is that clubs feel pressure to sell a player at a relatively early stage, for fear that he will otherwise leave on a free transfer. To be clear: this is not to say that the total of all transfer fees has fallen since 1995. On the contrary, it has risen. But that is because all the clubs now have more money than they did in 1995. However, total transfer fees would have been higher still if there had been no Bosman ruling.

The ruling has ensured that the big clubs can more easily lure good players away from the small clubs. As a result, the most talented players tend to move to the big clubs at a younger age. The ruling hits the poor clubs hardest; they receive less money from transfers than would have been the case without the ruling. This makes it hard for those clubs to maintain the quality of their sides, because they need a lot of money to pay today's high player wages. Sometimes clubs overcome the problem of the Bosman ruling with long-term contracts. But these can also work to their disadvantage: if a player fails to fulfil his promise his club may nevertheless have to continue paying his wages for years. All in all, the ruling has weakened the transfer system and it has added to the competitive inequality.

Since 1995 there have been some other, smaller changes in the transfer system as a result of pressure from the EU. For instance, the EU, FIFA and UEFA have agreed that the duration of a contract should be a maximum of five years. It has also been agreed that contracts have to be protected for a period of three years for players up to the age of twenty-eight, and two years for older players. Until now this rule has had little practical effect due to its vagueness; it is not clear exactly what the legal rights of club and player are when a player has served three years of a five-year contract, or two years if he is an older player. However, it is possible that, in such cases, the maximum transfer fee will become equal to the salary the player would have earned in the remaining years of his contract. This will have a downward effect on transfer fees, and so football will become a bit less competitive still, thanks to the EU.

Because a strict transfer system reduces competitive inequality, it would be sensible for the EU to change the law. The new law could ensure that clubs maintain the right to demand any transfer fee they wish for players with ongoing contracts. In addition, it may be worth allowing clubs the unilateral right to extend the contract of a player by one year, albeit only once. A proviso could be that the new salary is not lower than the old one. Alternatively, one could let the new salary be determined by an independent arbitrator. American baseball had such a system of salary arbitration for some time in the past, and it worked well. But these are details. The main point is that changing the law to make the transfer system more strict is sensible – unless still better methods can be found to reduce competitive inequality, a subject we will discuss later on.

However, to date, the EU does not want to consider changes to the law of the type proposed above, on the grounds that they conflict with the principle of free movement of workers, and thus also with the principle of a free European market. The EU cherishes such principles. It has always given them priority above other considerations, certainly in sport. To the EU, principles are more important than sports fans.

A FOREIGNER RULE

Throughout the history of professional football, football associations have imposed quotas on the number of foreigners a club is permitted to play. In the years just before 1995, most countries were using the three-plus-two rule: a club was allowed to have at most three foreigners on the field, plus two players who were also foreign but had played for at least five years in the domestic league. This issue also came up during the Jean-Marc Bosman case, because Bosman was a Belgian who wanted to play in France. On this point, too, the Court's verdict was clear: there must be no quotas for players from within the EU. The Court again cited the principle of free movement of workers within the EU, laid down in European Treaty rules. Since then, quotas have only been applied to players from outside the European Union.

Since 1995, many countries have seen a large increase in the number of foreign players, and much of this would not have been possible if the three-plus-two rule had remained in existence. Of course, rich clubs from large countries have obtained the best players. Smaller countries like Belgium and the Netherlands have seen all their stars move to countries like England, Germany and Spain, often at a young age. This development has increased competitive imbalance in European competitions. This comes as no surprise; when big clubs no longer face restrictions on nationality, they are no longer forced to field lesser players from their own country.

Many in the world of football are actually in favour of the reintroduction of a strict foreigner rule. One argument is that it reduces international competitive imbalances. Another is that many supporters appreciate seeing at least some fellow countrymen playing for their club.

So, in 2008, the international football federation FIFA decided that every club side in the world must have at least six players of its own nationality from 2012. This decision enjoyed broad support. UEFA was in favour, as were Franz Beckenbauer, Guus Hiddink and many other prominent individuals. Of the Dutch people, 72 per cent were in favour, with only 9 per cent against. The trouble is, the FIFA decision flies in the face of the Bosman ruling and runs counter to European law. Therefore, the European Commission has opposed it and, as a result, FIFA's foreigner rule was not adopted in 2012.

In 2014 FIFA announced a new attempt to get the rule implemented. But it will have little chance as long as the EU sticks to its old policy of maintaining the existing law, which it is expected to do.

However, laws are not sacrosanct. Why don't European politicians seek to amend the law if it will benefit sport, or if the population wants it? Of course, amendments to the law require the agreement of all member states and that is not easy to achieve. But with negotiation, and perhaps some give and take on different policy areas, a lot can be achieved. It was hard to get all the eurozone countries to agree on the Stability Pact, which bound them to make major cuts. But agree they did, partly because prominent politicians actively supported the Pact. If political problems can be overcome for a programme of cuts, they can also be overcome for a sensible sports policy. Or is the EU first and foremost a project for stimulating the free market and reducing government expenditure?

The European Commission has further justified its rejection of the 2008 FIFA plan by pointing to its discriminatory character. That sounds convincing. But the tournaments for national teams are even more discriminatory. Not a single foreigner is allowed to play for the English national side. Shouldn't this be prohibited too? The England team belongs to the English clubs, via the FA. It generates a lot of income and its players earn good money. It is therefore an economic activity. This means that, in principle, the rule of free movement of workers within the EU applies. The European law might therefore also imply that only a single European team should be allowed to play at the World Cup.

When it comes to national sides, however, the law is not strictly applied. Fortunately so – people enjoy watching their national team because they can identify with it. And if you are enthusiastic about your own team, you are likely to be interested in the opposition, or the country in which the matches are taking place. The World Cup is a meeting place for different countries and cultures. Moreover, it matters little to national fans whether their players are white, brown or black. The World Cup, of which discrimination on the basis of nationality is the core, stimulates understanding between races and cultures.

Essentially, in club football, the same considerations apply. Supporters want to be able to identify with their clubs. That is what makes football fun. It certainly helps if the club fields some players from its own region or country, which is why it is such a shame that the law is applied so strictly to club football.

Globalization confronts us with international competition and powerful multinationals. The EU helps us to cope with them. The common market has prepared us for ever-fiercer competition from outside Europe, and the EU has some power in the world. Good. But globalization also means that people need to have the self-confidence to be open to what comes from outside. Self-confidence is often linked to one's own identity and to strong roots in a familiar environment. For this reason, and others, the EU also needs to encourage countries and regions to preserve their identities.

Football can help here. A local club gives people something to belong to, and it can help them to be open to the rest of the world. The inhabitants of Twente – a region in the east of the Netherlands – are proud of their FC Twente. The club's all-time top scorer is the Swiss player, Blaise N'Kufo, who left the club in 2010. N'Kufo was, during his playing days, the most popular player with the fans, and he still generates affection today. He would also have been popular if FC Twente had played eleven foreigners in his time, but the club would have had fewer supporters then. That would have been bad for the region and for the way in which its people coped with globalization.

The principles of the free market and non-discrimination should not always be strictly applied. The market does not always work well, certainly not in the case of football, and too little individual character only leads to more rancour. As the German writer Goethe said: if you are always consistent, you end up with the devil.

LESSONS FROM AMERICA

We have seen that the 1960 All-Sports World Series was won by Europe with quite a satisfying score. Still, there are some things we can learn from the Americans, especially when it comes to competitive balance. As you will recall, America has three major team sports: baseball, basketball and American football. Each sport has a closed top league of around thirty clubs, and most clubs have commercial owners. What measures have they introduced to promote uncertainty of outcome?

The baseball clubs had already introduced a transfer system by 1879. Until 1976, it worked as follows. A player who was contracted to a club was not allowed to leave without his club's permission. The club retained the unilateral right to extend his contract, as long as his salary was not reduced. If a player were transferred, the new club might have to pay the old one a transfer fee, just like in Europe. But often the old club would be paid in players or rights to talented young players. A player could also be transferred against his will; the American baseball entrepreneurs knew how to play hard. When basketball and American football were on the rise they introduced the same kind of transfer system too.

The baseball clubs introduced the transfer system back in the 1870s because it reduced their ability to bid against each other for good players. This pushed down salary costs, so that losses were avoided and profits increased. For this reason above all others, the clubs have always remained in favour of the transfer system. However, they tend not to say so explicitly in public. Instead, the clubs have always emphasized that the system reduces competitive imbalance.

After 1976, the transfer systems in the three sports became less stringent, although all remain stricter than the current system in European football. For instance, in baseball, players who join a club will not be free agents for six years. After that, they are allowed to leave on a free transfer for a single transfer period, after which they are again not free to go for several years, and so on.

All three sports also have a 'rookie draft'. The teams that finish bottom of the league are allowed first pick of the most talented players from the lower leagues. The players themselves have little say in the matter. That weakens their negotiating position and moderates their salaries – which is precisely why the system was introduced. To the outside world, however, the clubs emphasize that it makes the weak teams stronger.

Another important instrument is revenue sharing. One type of revenue sharing concerns the gate receipts, of which a proportion goes to the away club in some sports. But the sharing of TV revenue is more important. In every sport, the league sells the TV rights for all matches to the national broadcasters, before sharing the proceeds equally between the clubs. In this way, even the small clubs get a lot of money. The clubs emphasize that this increases uncertainty of outcome, but what also counts for them is that it increases profits. There are at least two reasons for this. First, the league acts as a monopoly when it sells all the TV rights, so that the clubs do not compete with each other in selling the rights of their own matches. That helps to increase the price. Second, whatever happens, every club gets a lot of money, even if it frequently loses, thereby reducing the need to pay players high wages, and so lowering the costs of the club.

So all the measures above have increased profits, but although the clubs like to say in public that they reduce competitive imbalance, this is much less certain. Quite a few economists assert that the transfer system and the rookie draft do not reduce the imbalances. And there are also economists who assert that the same holds true for revenue sharing. However, opinions differ about these conclusions. For us, what is important is that they are based on one crucial assumption: clubs are only motivated by profit – so that, when a measure improves the position of small clubs, their owners may use this for attaining higher profits rather than a stronger squad. The conclusions are therefore somewhat less relevant for Europe, where – certainly outside England – most clubs are primarily interested in on-field success. So in Europe, a strict transfer system can still increase uncertainty of outcome. Indeed, this is what has been argued earlier in this chapter. Whether or not revenue sharing is sensible for Europe will be discussed later. But before that, we had better learn something more from the Americans.

GREAT AMERICAN INVENTIONS

The Americans are a creative people. Their footprints are on the moon. They invented the tractor, the aeroplane and the jukebox. More recently, they brought us Windows, Google, the salary cap and the luxury tax. Never heard of that? Time to wake up!

In 1984, the Americans introduced a new instrument in basketball: the salary cap. This is how it worked in its early years. First, the average income of the clubs in the top division was calculated. Each club was then allowed to spend a maximum of 53 per cent of that amount on player salaries, with a minimum of 47 per cent. Today, basketball still has a similar type of cap. American football also has a salary cap.

What are the results of such salary caps, if strictly enforced? Well, especially the richer clubs will have to curtail their team payroll, or in other words, their spending on player salaries. Taken by itself, this will increase their profits. However, the minimum for the team payroll can have the opposite effect for weaker clubs. In relation to this and some other points, the effects on league-wide profits are uncertain. With regard to competitive imbalance, the situation is simpler: as long as the difference between the minimum and the maximum is sufficiently low, all clubs will spend approximately the same amount on players. That will make the competition close.

Unfortunately, there are all kinds of official exceptions to the rule. In addition, clubs use tricks to evade the official rules. As a result, the large clubs still spend much more on players than the small ones. Indeed, there is no evidence that the cap in basketball has reduced competitive inequality. Even in American football, where there are fewer exceptions, there is, as yet, no convincing evidence that the cap has had a serious effect on competitive inequality – although perhaps it has decreased a bit.

Still, the basic idea is a good one, and one day the practical problems may be solved so that the true value of this invention will be fully revealed.

The 'luxury tax' was introduced by baseball in 1997, and basketball followed in 1999. The details of the schemes have varied over the years. The 2013 luxury tax for baseball is a good example. In 2013, every Major League Baseball club that spent more than 178 million dollars on players had to pay a tax on the excess to the organizers of the league. The tax rate was 17.5 per cent of the excess if the club had not exceeded the threshold in the previous year, and much higher otherwise. Only the New York Yankees and the Los Angeles Dodgers had a team payroll in excess of 178 million dollars, and so only these two teams paid the tax in 2013. The Yankees paid about 29 million dollars, the Dodgers 10 million. In basketball, the number of clubs that exceed the threshold and pay the tax tends to be higher.

The proceeds of the luxury tax go to various parties, depending on the sport. Important beneficiaries can be the (other) clubs, the players and the league organizers. And in baseball, some of the proceeds are used to develop the sport in other countries. It is hoped this will also increase the future revenues of the American clubs.

The luxury tax, too, can decrease competitive inequality, if well enforced. The reason is simple: the tax makes it more costly for rich clubs to attract top players by paying them high salaries, thus reducing their incentive to do so.

Since the luxury tax is a recent phenomenon, there is little evidence yet about its effects in practice. In earlier years, the schemes were such that the amount paid by the biggest clubs was small, so that the effects on competitive inequality may also have been small. Still, the instrument may well hold serious promise.

HOW TO GET THINGS DONE

The Americans have quite a few measures in place which, ostensibly at least, are designed to increase uncertainty of outcome, and which can sometimes do just that. How have they managed to get so many measures implemented and keep most of them in force?

To begin with, it is necessary for the clubs to agree among themselves to introduce a new measure. A top league in America has about thirty clubs and those are always the same. This makes negotiating a lot more straightforward, although not necessarily easy. Some measures, such as the luxury tax, directly involve the rich clubs losing money, and the official intention of all measures is to make the big clubs lose more games, and some measures may indeed have such an effect in practice. Losing games is not only undesirable in sporting terms, but it can also lead to reduced income in the short term. So the big clubs won't always be lining up to applaud. But there are benefits for them too. First, as discussed above, the measures can have positive effects on profits even if they do not reduce competitive imbalances. And second, a closer competition may be good for the revenue of all clubs in the long term, including the big ones. After all, a club that always wins will eventually attract fewer spectators. For these reasons, the clubs have often managed to reach an agreement.

But there are other obstacles. Many measures are at odds with the ideals of a free market and fair competition, and hence with competition law. In 1914, a number of baseball clubs that had been refused entry to the Major League went to court, alleging, among other things, that the transfer system acted to obstruct the labour market and was therefore illegal. This ultimately led to a ruling by the American Supreme Court in 1922. The Court's verdict was far-reaching: it ruled that baseball fell completely outside competition law. The ruling attracted a lot of criticism, but it remained in force, in part because the legislature refused to change the law and so invalidate the ruling.

American football and basketball were never placed outside of competition law. This left them exposed to the risk of legal action. In 1953, the National Football League sold the rights to broadcast all matches in the top league to a particular TV station. In doing so, lawyers claimed, the league was operating as a cartel to force up the price, which was illegal. Instead, every club ought to sell its broadcasting rights separately. The clubs feared being sued and started lobbying for a law that would permit the joint sale of TV rights. Their argument was that the revenue was divided equally between the clubs, so making the league more competitive. The clubs' lobbying was successful: in 1962, Congress approved a law to this effect, precisely with a view to reducing competitive imbalance. The same law was extended to cover basketball.

In American football and basketball there was also a real risk that the courts would prohibit the transfer system under competition law. And aside from competition law, the system appeared to conflict with other legislation, particularly in the sphere of employment law. Even baseball was at risk in this regard. Court cases were launched and many were lost by the clubs. But they only related to parts of the system; the fundamentals remained intact for a long time.

This was due, above all, to the fact that few players took their clubs to court. The players were afraid. A player who took his club to court could be blacklisted, which would mean never playing in the top league again.

When a top league has only a limited number of clubs, it has a limited number of players as well, which makes it easy for them to organize themselves. Each sport formed a union for all the players in the top league. Around 1970, those unions turned their sights on the respective transfer systems. They launched court cases on behalf of whole groups of players at a time. The clubs could hardly blacklist all those players. The prospect of the transfer system being dismantled loomed.

This outcome was ultimately avoided. The law could be applied less strictly if employers and employees could agree with each other. So the clubs sat down with the unions. The unions were also wary of scrapping the transfer system. They feared a large supply of transfer-free players and lower salaries as a result. Compromises were reached. Each sport put in place a new transfer system that was better for the players, but still reasonably strict.

Later, the clubs came up with a proposal for a salary cap. In basketball and American football, the unions agreed, primarily because the cap was coupled with a minimum amount for the team payroll. More generally, for the past four decades, clubs and unions in each sport have sat down together to agree policy measures in all kinds of areas. Those agreements remain in force for a number of years before being renegotiated. Often the negotiations go reasonably smoothly because both parties need each other. The clubs cannot do without their star players, and the players need the clubs and their stadiums. In this way, each gets his share.

Even so, negotiations can become deadlocked, sometimes resulting in player strikes. In 1994, one such strike brought Major League Baseball to a standstill for eight months. In turn, the clubs sometimes back up their demands with lockouts: no matches organized, no wages. The longest was in the 1998–99 season, when the length of the basketball league season was cut by half, to the great sadness of fans. But then, the fans don't have a seat at the negotiating table.

All in all, there are three reasons why America has so many measures to enhance uncertainty of outcome. The top leagues have few clubs, which makes it easier for them to reach agreements and lobby the government effectively. The authorities, including the courts, have been tolerant. And there are unions to conclude agreements with the clubs, which makes the courts even more accommodating. Americans know how to get things done.

EUROPEANS ARE LESS SOCIAL NOW

We can now compare the three major American team sports with our European football and see what we can learn from that. Let us start with revenue sharing. This instrument is important in America, but it is also widespread in European football. In many European countries, TV rights for matches in the national league are sold by a central organization that shares out the proceeds between the clubs. In some cases this is the national football association. In other cases it is a body representing the clubs in a particular division, such as the Premier League. At European level, UEFA often acts as the central sales organization.

In sharing out the proceeds from central sales, the guiding principle has always been that the small clubs get more than they would be entitled to if only their viewing figures are taken into account. This has tended to reduce competitive inequality, certainly in the past – which has always been the argument put forward by the football clubs for permitting the joint sale of TV images, even if it seems to be at odds with competition law. The argument has generally been accepted by the courts.

So there are some similarities with America, but there are also differences, and they have become more apparent in modern times. In Europe, the proceeds from joint sales are not usually divided entirely equally between the clubs, certainly not today – unlike the TV rights sold to national broadcasters in the US. On our side of the pond, the trend over the years has been for TV income to gradually be divided less equally.

There is an explanation for this. The European cup competitions have become increasingly important over the past fifty years, certainly in financial terms. In connection with this, in many countries, the best clubs have increasingly objected to an all-too-equal distribution of the national TV pot. These clubs do not deny that such a distribution makes the national league more interesting. However, they place more emphasis on a different consideration: if the best clubs in the country get too little from the national pot, they can buy fewer good players and so they will win less often in European tournaments. For instance, for Ajax it no longer makes sense to contribute too much to making the Dutch league more competitive through the distribution of TV money, because if the club goes down that road, it will lose in Europe more often.

When it comes to sharing out the TV income from the Champions League, in one sense the problem is reversed. In this case, if the money were to be equally divided among the participants, those from smaller countries would receive so much that they would be able to dominate their own national leagues almost completely. That could mean, for instance, the championship of Greece always being won by the same club. It is difficult, if not impossible, to conceive of a system for the distribution of TV money that would make both the European tournaments and the national leagues more competitive. And even if such a system were conceivable, it probably would not be introduced. This is because agreement would have to be reached with hundreds of clubs from many different countries and leagues – a near-impossible task.

In conclusion, revenue sharing does not particularly suit the European league structure as it exists today. The importance of the measure will therefore continue to wane. The past is the past.

AN AMERICAN SALARY CAP FOR BAYERN MUNICH?

The American salary cap is aimed at ensuring that the clubs in the top league all spend roughly the same amount on players. There are serious enforcement problems, but the principle is clear: when expenditure on player salaries does not depend on income, competitive inequality as caused by differences in financial strength will disappear. It is worth asking whether this American invention can help European football.

But what should the principle be in Europe? European football has both national and European competitions. In order to make the Champions League more competitive, Bayern Munich should have a salary cap which equals that of Celtic. To make the Scottish League more competitive, Celtic's cap should be the same as St Mirren's. Having both caps at the same time wouldn't make sense, because then Bayern Munich would be just as strong as St Mirren, so an American-style salary cap is not a serviceable instrument for European football. As far as that goes, the closed American top leagues, with their simple formats, have an advantage: there, the measure can work in principle.

It is also probable that a European salary cap would immediately be ruled illegal by the courts. In the United States, the salary cap, in both American football and basketball, is based on an agreement between the clubs and the union representing all the players in the top league.

It is these agreements that have made the courts so accommodating. Without them, the caps would probably have been banned long ago, because they would be at odds with the ideals of a free market, and hence with American law.

European law does not really differ from US law in this regard. But Europe does not have a strong union representing all professional footballers. There are many different leagues in Europe and tens of thousands of professional players with a great range of abilities. This makes it nigh on impossible to establish a union that can negotiate with the clubs on sweeping measures on behalf of all players. And without agreement between players and clubs, the courts would probably never permit a salary cap.

To summarize, an American-style salary cap would not suit the structure of European competitions. Such a cap could only be of use to Europe if we were to change our league structure. But that is a matter for later. For the time being, let us simply say that the Americans have created something which can be good for them, but Europe must do what is appropriate to Europe.

GO YOUR OWN WAY

So, an American-style salary cap is not suitable for the European league system. But there is still that other American invention which might be a source of inspiration for our old continent: the luxury tax.

Many people think that the American culture is one in which socialism is unpopular. But when it comes to sport, the Americans were the first to see that part of the money earned by the richest clubs could be seen as a luxury, as money not really needed, and so they introduced the luxury tax. Of course, they have designed their luxury tax in such a way that it suits the American top leagues, which have only some thirty clubs. Their luxury tax has one threshold level, and only the few clubs with a team payroll in excess of the threshold pay the tax.

The league system of European football, with more than a thousand clubs, is more complicated, and therefore an American-type luxury tax is not the best possible instrument. Of course, we could have a luxury tax for team payrolls in excess of, say, 100 million euros. This would mean that just a few European clubs would pay the tax. This would help make the Champions League somewhat more interesting and the Premier League too. But for most national leagues there would be no effect on competitive inequality. For instance, the payrolls of the best Dutch clubs are not even half of 100 million euros, so they would pay nothing at all. Therefore, in the next section, we will investigate whether or not it is possible to have some variant of the luxury tax which better suits the European league system.

But for now, the time has come for words of goodbye. I would like to thank our American friends for the insights they have brought us. We have come to admire their great entrepreneurial spirit, which has made somewhat boring sports like baseball so amazingly popular in their own country. Certainly, we shall never forget the sporting vision and dreams of baseball lover Bill Veeck, that brilliant businessman with an ashtray built into his wooden leg. And with all the inspiration men like him have given us, we will now investigate the dream of letting European football be European again.

A PROGRESSIVE SOCIAL LEVY

Earlier in the book, attention was paid to the concept of a flat social levy. With this levy, each club would be required to spend 10 per cent of its team payroll on social projects. It was argued that this would improve economic welfare, while making the game more social.

But to make European football more competitive, we need a progressive social levy. Like the flat social levy, it is applied to the team payroll. The first 2 million euros spent on players' wages in a season are exempt from the levy. For the next 4 million of the payroll, the levy is 5 per cent. On the next four, the percentage is somewhat higher, and so on. The biggest clubs pay a levy of, say, 90 per cent of the final millions they spend on players' wages. As with the flat social levy, every club can spend the proceeds on social projects as it sees fit. Perhaps part of the proceeds can go to national sports associations, which will have sufficient opportunities to use the money well.

To illustrate, let me give some rough estimates. If the levy had been introduced in the 2012–13 season, the total levy for Manchester United could have amounted to, say, 105 million euros, or some 90 billion pounds. This would have equalled about 50 per cent of the payroll, or 25 per cent of the club's total revenues. The levy for Celtic would have been around 6 million pounds, or 18 per cent of the payroll. That for St Mirren could have been 25,000 pounds, or 1 per cent of the payroll.

So the richest clubs face by far the biggest levy. Therefore, the amount they can pay players net of the levy falls strongly. As a result, it becomes harder for them to lure good players away from other clubs, and so Celtic will stand a better chance of beating Manchester United, and St Mirren will score more goals against Celtic.

The instrument is based on the same elementary idea as the American luxury tax: taxation can be an instrument for increasing uncertainty of outcome. However, the luxury tax concerns the income above one single, high-threshold level only, so that only a few clubs have to pay. The progressive levy applies to small clubs too, while its rate gradually increases to make the richer clubs in particular pay a very high amount. This makes the instrument suitable for Europe, with its many clubs of all sizes playing in different but connected competitions. And the revenues of this instrument are used entirely for social purposes, instead of being mainly used to help smaller clubs, league organizers and players – as is the case with the luxury tax.

But aren't a lot of clubs already strapped for cash? They can't suddenly start diverting large sums of money to social projects, can they? By this reasoning, the proposal might seem to be a non-starter. But we can also reason differently. These days, professional football generates much more revenue than it did fifty years ago. Viewed this way, the clubs ought to have money to spare. Which of these is the right way to look at it?

One thing has never changed: the average club barely turns a profit. Increased income is set against a roughly equal increase in costs. This is largely the result of players' wages. A club that earns more money will try to buy better players and that means paying higher wages. But all clubs have increased their earnings, so all clubs are paying more, and so wages have risen across the board. The progressive social levy will instead curb all clubs' abilities to pay high wages (net of the levy), leading to an overall reduction in wages and therefore costs, so the clubs will not go bust.

Indeed, this is the old economic rent argument used earlier for the flat 10 per cent social levy. It also applies here, even though the levy is higher now for the rich clubs. But this should be no problem, since economic rent in football is really very high. In 2013 Manchester United earned (in real terms) 158 times as much as the English champion of 1960, Burnley. If it loses 25 per cent of its income through the levy, it can still earn more than 119 times as much as Burnley did in 1960. Wouldn't that be enough?

Of course, the levy should be announced well in advance and be introduced gradually. This would give clubs time to adjust wages downwards. The FFP rules can help them to do this. The players will make less money, but the better ones will still become millionaires. And football, which owes its success to all the volunteers who helped develop the game in the past, will return to its social and typically European roots.

Will UEFA introduce a levy like this of its own accord? UEFA is concerned about the increased predictability of match outcomes, but it has not proposed any fundamental measures to meet this concern. We will discuss the reasons for this later on. For now, let us not expect too much from UEFA.

If the football sector fails to act, that leaves the authorities. Here we come back to the EU. When a problem is cross-border in nature, there can be a role for it, and this is now the case in football. Football clubs compete with each other at European level, across national borders. For this reason, there would be little point in only Scotland introducing a progressive levy; that would just mean AC Milan beating Celtic more easily still. The levy must be imposed by the EU, in cooperation with UEFA, and possibly also Russia. Naturally, there are also good clubs in South America, but they are not as rich and cannot lure top European players away from us. For this reason, Europe could easily impose a high levy.

If the European countries can agree, every measure that benefits football can be introduced. But do the authorities really want to help the football fans?

SADDER BUT WISER

In present times, there are not many measures left to reduce competitive imbalances in Europe. The transfer system has been emasculated by the Bosman ruling to a significant extent, and risks becoming even less effective in the future. On account of that same ruling, the foreigner rule now applies only to players from outside the EU. Television revenue sharing is becoming less effective, as the big clubs receive an ever bigger slice of the pie.

Why are there so few effective measures left? One reason is the attitude of the EU, which adheres strictly to the ideal of the free market. This ideal is also applied to the labour market; employees must always be free to change jobs. Now the free market may work well in many parts of the economy, but in professional team sports, the market has a serious drawback: it increases competitive inequality. European administrators and judges have lost sight of this fact, in contrast with their American counterparts. This has been the reason for the weakening of the transfer system. The EU also elevates another ideal above any other consideration: no discrimination on the basis of nationality. This has led to the scrapping of the foreigner rule for European players.

A second cause is the complicated league system of European football, which includes both national and European competitions. In this system a fundamental problem has arisen with the revenue-sharing instrument. Sharing income at the national level can have the effect of wrecking the chances of the country's best teams in European matches; sharing out the income from European matches among the clubs playing these matches can reduce the competitiveness of some of the national leagues. Due to this problem, revenue sharing is becoming steadily less useful. The introduction of an American-style salary cap in European football can be ruled out for similar reasons. Of course, we could consider the possibility of changing the league system, but we have not yet reached that subject.

There are two new measures that would effectively increase uncertainty of outcome throughout the European league system: a pay-

TV ban and a progressive social levy. These measures would have to be taken at the European level. However, it is doubtful whether UEFA would ever introduce any of them of its own volition. UEFA can implement radical changes only if its 'membership' agrees. That membership consists of dozens of national football associations and well over a thousand clubs. This alone makes it very difficult to get all the football associations and clubs, or at least most of them, to agree. Moreover, as will be discussed further later on, the big clubs have the greatest influence, and they are the ones who are least concerned about the problem of competitive imbalance. What they want is to become stronger themselves. Understandably so – after all, who wouldn't want to win important prizes?

In a situation like that, government intervention can make sense, but to date, the authorities in Europe have done practically nothing. The thinking has always been that the market works reasonably well for football and the authorities should intervene as little as possible, and if there are problems, the football sector should preferably solve them itself. Politicians like to point to the benefits of 'self-regulation', which apparently absolves them of responsibility to do anything themselves. The trouble is, the football authorities are all too passive these days, and so football becomes less and less exciting to watch. The more you think about it, the sadder it is. Certainly if you are Dutch!

5

THE LEAGUE SYSTEM

SILVIO BERLUSCONI AND RUPERT MURDOCH

In 1998, the Milan-based company Media Partners put forward a plan for a new football competition, the Super League. It held secret discussions with sixteen leading European clubs, among whom were Manchester United, Liverpool, Real Madrid, Barcelona, AC Milan, Bayern Munich, Paris Saint-Germain and Ajax. As a result of the secrecy, it was not immediately clear quite what the intention was.

According to plans later made public, at least sixteen and possibly thirty-two clubs would have taken part in the Super League. And, in any case, the plan would have been to designate at least sixteen clubs that could never be relegated from the Super League. The new competition would have involved more matches than the existing European cup competitions. Those matches would have taken place in midweek, allowing the participants to play in their national leagues at the weekend. In this way, the Super League would have represented an alternative to UEFA's European cup competitions. At the same time, the national leagues would have been devalued; some clubs would always be allowed to play in the Super League and would therefore no longer need their national leagues to qualify for European football. There were also rumours that Media Partners did not actually want the participants to play nationally at all, and that Super League matches would also have taken place at weekends.

Behind Media Partners were four financiers: Silvio Berlusconi, Rupert Murdoch, Leo Kirch and the Saudi prince Al-Waleed bin Talal. The latter was keen to invest his petrodollars in profitable projects, while the other three were well-known media magnates. Kirch died in 2011, but Berlusconi and Murdoch are still active. Berlusconi is the owner of popular Italian TV stations and numerous other companies, including AC Milan. Murdoch has owned Sky Television for years and, with him, English football has led the way in pay TV.

Berlusconi and Murdoch have always had warm relations with leading politicians. Berlusconi has even been a politician himself, acting as Italy's prime minister for nine years in total. Unfortunately, the two media tycoons have not really had good relations with the legal system. Berlusconi was hit hardest by the judiciary: in 2013, he got a four-year prison sentence for tax fraud. Because of an amnesty aimed at reducing prison overcrowding, the effective sentence was reduced to one year and, because he is an older man, he does not have to go to jail but must do community service for four hours a week for one year. (It is not entirely clear whether these four hours will include a coffee break.)

Back to 1998. Why did Media Partners try to organize a football competition? An important reason was that it was interested in securing the TV rights to the Super League, which were expected to generate a fortune. The business model of the Super League would have been based on pay TV. At that time, pay TV had yet to become popular in most countries, either in football or further afield. Murdoch had previously said that he regarded sports as the 'battering ram' for pay TV, and it seemed that with the Super League he had brought the battering ram into a good position.

At the time, I feared that the organizers of the Super League were only going to choose sixteen clubs and that Ajax would be the only Dutch team to be invited to join the Super League. I also feared that promotion to the Super League would not be part of the final plan, so that my club, Feyenoord, would remain a second-class club forever. And so, although I disliked the plan, I hoped that, if it went through, there would be thirty-two clubs in the Super League – since that would have meant that Feyenoord, with its large fan base, would also be allowed in. And I would, albeit reluctantly, have accepted the consequence: with thirty-two clubs, PSV Eindhoven and all other Dutch clubs would not be invited to join the Super League and remain second-class clubs forever. So I was opposed to the plan, but my main concern was that my club was going to play at the highest level. First things first.

Perhaps this was exactly how Murdoch and Berlusconi wanted people like me to think. Businessmen like them often exploit rivalries. To illustrate this with one other example: Murdoch's pay-TV channel generates a great deal of money for English clubs, increasing their chances of beating clubs from abroad. Thus, it is an advantage for the English fans that subscription fees are high in their country. Sooner or later, that advantage will come to an end, as pay TV spreads to other countries. At that point, Murdoch will probably find new ways to help the English teams, such as further increasing subscription fees, perhaps. Divide and make money, that's the strategy.

So when Media Partners proposed the original plan for a Super League, it was using the same strategy – by, among other things, organizing secret meetings to which some clubs were invited and other clubs were not. Rupert Murdoch and Silvio Berlusconi wanted each club to walk alone.

Back to the main story. In 1998, Media Partners tried to convince a small number of top clubs of the benefits of the Super League, and offered them huge sums for their TV rights. Initially, the attempt appeared to be successful, as most of the sixteen clubs invited looked set to back the plan.

Yet it failed. UEFA refused to let itself be sidelined just like that. It realized that it had to accommodate the rich clubs and, in response, it set up its own working group, which included representatives from the clubs that were negotiating with Media Partners. The working group quickly reached an agreement: the Champions League was expanded from twenty-four to thirty-two clubs, with a structure that would tend towards increased participation by rich clubs from the big countries. In addition, the division of TV money was modified, again in favour of the rich clubs.

Media Partners had lost. But one of its founders, Berlusconi, wasn't too concerned. His club, AC Milan, actually benefited from the developments – as did all the other rich clubs. Since 1998, it has been clear who holds the power in football: the rich clubs.

A TRUE SUPER LEAGUE

Although the Media Partners initiative was torpedoed, a Super League may, nevertheless, appear in the long run. And when it happens, it will probably be a competition with so many matches that the participants will no longer be able to play in their national leagues: a true Super League, in other words.

Today, the competitive imbalances between clubs are getting bigger. There are ever fewer clubs that stand a reasonable chance of reaching the semi-finals of the Champions League. So for clubs that no longer have much of a chance, such as clubs from Portugal or Greece, the tournament has become less enjoyable than it used to be. But even the genuine contenders face a problem: the matches they play in the autumn against the weaker sides are gradually becoming less exciting. In national leagues, uncertainty of outcome is also often waning.

So the attractiveness of many matches is threatened by the increasing competitive inequality. For the dwindling band of top European clubs, therefore, the idea of playing more matches against each other is becoming increasingly attractive, because those matches are always competitive. For this reason, some sports economists have argued that a Super League may well emerge in the long term, or is even inevitable. Let's follow their line of thinking for a moment.

What will be the form of a new Super League then? Some sports economists have put forward a proposal for a competition which, to a large extent, resembles the top American competitions. A difference is that, in their proposal, the Super League for European football would number sixty clubs, whereas the US Major Leagues have only around thirty teams in each sport. But as in the US, the clubs would always be the same; relegation would be impossible. The sixty clubs would be divided between four regional divisions: North, South-West, Central and East.

Division North, for instance, would consist of six clubs from England, three from the Netherlands, two from Scotland and one each from Denmark, Norway, Sweden and Finland. The six English teams would most likely include Manchester United, Liverpool, Chelsea and Arsenal. The two remaining places would be allocated primarily on the basis of commercial considerations, such as the size of a club's support. The two participants from Scotland would undoubtedly be Celtic and Rangers.

The fifteen clubs in Division North would play each other twice a season. That would give each club twenty-eight matches to start with. In addition, each club would play eighteen matches against clubs from the other three regional divisions, bringing the total to forty-six matches. The points gained by a club after those forty-six matches would determine its final position in Division North. The club on top would be the champions of Northern Europe.

These champions, together with the clubs placed second, third and fourth in Division North, would go into the play-offs to decide the champions of Europe. There they would play against the best teams from the other three divisions. The play-offs, and the season, would end with the final to decide the European title.

Of course, the Super League may well end up taking a slightly different form to that sketched out here. For example, a league of thirty-two clubs is also a possibility, and there may also be promotion and relegation to and from the Super League.

Whatever its exact form, a Super League would reduce the inequalities between the participating clubs, among other things, because they would always be playing in the same league. For example, Celtic would no longer suffer the disadvantage of playing in the Scottish league while AC Milan played in the more lucrative Italian league; as a result, Celtic would stand a better chance against Milan.

In addition, there are two potentially important measures for reducing competitive imbalances – an American-style salary cap and revenue sharing – which are particularly well-suited to a closed competition such as the Super League. As explained earlier, these measures are poorly suited to our present league system, because they can never make the European tournaments and the national leagues simultaneously more competitive. However, in the Super League they would work in one direction only: to increase uncertainty of outcome in all matches.

Of course, there are other measures that could make the present system more exciting. A stricter transfer system or a progressive social levy for instance. But Europe makes little use of such measures. We discussed the reasons for this earlier. One of the reasons is that UEFA can do little on its own. It has a membership of dozens of national football associations and well over a thousand clubs. That alone makes agreement on sweeping measures difficult to achieve. Moreover, the thirty richest clubs have the greatest influence within UEFA, and they have little interest in supporting the hundreds of poor clubs just so that they will lose more matches themselves.

In that sense, the Super League has an advantage. No more than sixty clubs would take part, which would make agreements much easier to reach. Of course, the richest clubs will never allow all clubs to become as strong as themselves. But just as in the US, the richest clubs in a closed top competition in Europe will come to favour measures that make the sport more competitive, at least to a certain degree. This is, first, because a Super League of sixty clubs would have only a limited number of 'weaker' clubs that needed support from the richer clubs. Second, a more competitive league would lead to higher income for all participants. And third, so America teaches us, there are various measures aimed at increasing uncertainty of outcome that also tend to – or indeed are primarily designed to – improve the financial positions of the clubs. Salary caps are a clear example. All in all, it is likely that the Super League would include measures that reduce competitive inequality, and so it may be pretty exciting.

Which has to be a good thing, doesn't it?

WHAT THE FANS WANT

We have seen that, if current developments continue, matches in the existing league system will become less competitive and therefore less enjoyable. A new Super League would be fairly competitive, and in that sense it could at least then represent an improvement for many supporters.

But how would the comparison work out if we were to make the existing leagues more competitive? Since UEFA itself will not introduce appropriate measures to this end, such as a progressive social levy, the EU would have to impose them from above. Whether or not this is realistic will be discussed later on. For the time being, we will simply assume that the EU does actually force through such measures, making the existing leagues more competitive again. So Newcastle and Leeds United get a chance of winning the English title again, and Hamburger SV and Red Star Belgrade may win the most important European trophy once more.

The question then is, how would the existing league system with increased competitive balance compare with a competitive Super League? In our comparison, we will assume there is a Super League of sixty clubs, as described previously. While this Super League may be competitive, it will never be the case that all the participants will have an equal chance of becoming European champions. The bigger clubs will always have a better chance. But that also applies to the existing system.

Before continuing, it is emphasized that it is difficult to predict the future preferences of football fans. Therefore, the conclusion reached below should not be regarded as one that is certainly true, but as reflecting my view as an 'informed economist'. The underlying argument is given in short below, while the online supplement gives a more thorough analysis. Still, despite all my work, your view may be better than mine – at least, if you think about the arguments first.

So let's make the comparison between the existing league system with improved competitive balance and a competitive Super League. What will this Super League be like for an Ajax supporter? If the Amsterdammers are as lucky as they have been in the past – and they've been lucky quite a lot – then Ajax may become Super League champions once in every twenty years. In four out of those twenty years Ajax will still be in the title race until spring and they will reach the play-offs twice. For the other sixteen years, Ajax will be a mid-table side, with fixtures against Porto and Brøndby that have little importance from February onwards.

This picture is less attractive to Ajax fans than the prospect offered if the existing competitions are retained. In this case Ajax would, with their usual luck, win the Champions League once every twenty years and reach the quarter-finals in four other years. In addition, there may well be years in which the club goes a long way in UEFA's Europa League; perhaps Ajax will win that tournament now and again. On average, Ajax plays around ten European matches per season. This makes a match like that more unique, exciting and attractive than a match in the Super League, of which there will be forty-six in any one year at least. In addition, Ajax plays in the Dutch competition, which is often quite competitive and comes with all kinds of regional rivalries. On average, the Amsterdam club can expect to be involved in the title race until the spring in about sixteen out of twenty years, winning perhaps eight times. That means eight years with big celebrations for Ajax fans. And Ajax fans like their celebrations.

A critical note could be that (witness some excesses from the past) such celebrations may involve an arrogant Ajax coach standing on a platform and loudly proclaiming that Ajax is not only the best club in the Netherlands and the best club in Amsterdam, but also the best club in Rotterdam. But let us forget such unpleasant details. We need to understand the bigger picture and rise above regional rivalries. Or, let me say it more clearly still: Ajax have won the European title more often than Feyenoord. And, yes, Ajax's Johan Cruijff was a better player than Feyenoord's beloved star midfielder Willem van Hanegem, and better than Robin van Persie too. When we are facing men like Murdoch and Berlusconi, we simply can no longer walk alone.

So, in cases where the existing competitions are made more competitive, the current competition set-up will be more appealing to Ajax fans than a Super League. And essentially the same will hold true for fans of clubs like Galatasaray and Glasgow Rangers, and also for supporters of somewhat bigger clubs like Arsenal and Dortmund.

If a Super League happens, Everton will probably not be part of it. Instead, it will be playing in an English league shorn of the six biggest English clubs. That will leave it with a good chance of winning, but it will be a denuded English championship. So, on balance, the Super League system will probably not be good for Everton fans. The same goes for supporters of clubs like Aberdeen, Werder Bremen and FC Twente.

All in all, the Super League will not be an improvement for the fans. The current system is more attractive, at least assuming measures are brought in to increase competitiveness again. The trouble is, it is not the supporters who decide these things.

DIFFERENT CLUBS

We now turn to the question of whether or not the clubs will want the Super League. The answer will depend on the type of club, and so the different types of club must be described first. To start with, there are big clubs and small clubs. Big clubs are those that will probably play in the proposed Super League. Small clubs probably won't.

Another distinction can be made between those clubs with a constitution that requires them to serve the interests of their fans, and those clubs which face no such restriction. The former are still in the majority. For instance, Barcelona and Real Madrid are associations that all supporters can join, and they elect the board. Elsewhere in Europe, the boards of the clubs are often chosen in different ways, but here, too, many boards are officially bound to serve the fans. The second group of clubs is different: they are owned by large companies, rich individuals or other shareholders. Such owners can pursue their own objectives. Some owners love football and want to give something to the fans. In those cases, the difference an association makes may be small. But other owners are mainly interested in making a profit.

Focusing on the big clubs, we see that many of them are officially bound to serve their fans, but their numbers are falling. This is logical. Every now and then, a profit-driven company or a rich individual takes over a big club, but the converse never happens – associations or supporters' trusts have never bought a big club from rich owners. They simply lack the money to do so. The trend can, therefore, only go in one direction: towards more big clubs that are profit-driven.

For the small clubs, the situation is different. Quite a few supporters' trusts have already shown that they can raise sufficient money to take over a small club, and the same may happen again in the future.

So the number of small clubs that are officially bound to serve their fans may not fall.

In 1998, when Media Partners was having secret negotiations with big European clubs about the formation of a Super League, there were rumours that the strongest opposition to the plan came from Barcelona and Real Madrid. The reason may have been that the boards of those clubs, which had been elected by the fans, were thinking more about the fans than about the money offered.

However, these are just rumours. You may not be interested in rumours and we have to think about the future. The big investors are also thinking deeply. And one question they may be pondering is this: is it possible to tear the different clubs apart?

WHAT DIFFERENT CLUBS WANT

The question now is whether or not a Super League is attractive for the different types of clubs. For the time being, we will continue to assume that measures are introduced to make the existing leagues more competitive. So how will the different clubs view a Super League in that case?

First, the small clubs. As we discussed earlier, their supporters will have less pleasure with the Super League system, as playing in a denuded national league is less appealing. And, because of this, the clubs will also see their revenues fall. So it makes no difference whether the club puts fans or profits first: a small club will always be against the new system.

Second, the big clubs. As argued previously, their supporters will also have less pleasure with a Super League. For this reason, big clubs that put their fans first will also be opposed to a Super League. That leaves the big profit-driven clubs. Their supporters will be against the Super League. However, that does not mean that participating in it will reduce the clubs' profits, causing the owners to be against it too. At first sight this may seem strange, so a longer explanation is needed here.

Most fans like to support a club from their own country, preferably a club with some chance of winning major honours. If England ends up with six clubs playing in a future Super League, then in the long term nearly every English football fan will be supporting one of these clubs (possibly alongside another local club). These six clubs will there- fore gain more supporters, and they will start charging higher prices, especially if they are profit-driven clubs. This much adheres to the standard economic insight, according to which profit-seeking entre- preneurs will charge higher prices when they have fewer competitors. After all, their customers are less likely to go elsewhere. So the English clubs in the Super League will see the ranks of their supporters swell and they will be charging them higher prices. As a result, their rev- enues will increase. The same will apply to Super League clubs from other countries.

Moreover, a Super League offers some other opportunities to make money. Specifically, as the US example shows, there are measures to reduce competitive imbalances, which also have the secondary or primary effect of increasing profits, and they are easier to get off the ground in a closed top competition. The salary cap is a good example here. So a Super League can boost profits in various ways.

On the other hand, the participants in the Super League will lose their fixtures in the popular national leagues. This will have a negative impact on their income and profits. It cannot be predicted whether this effect will exceed the positive effects; the reverse may also hold true. So we are left with much uncertainty about the effects of a Super League on profits.

The chance that the negative effect on profits exceeds the positive effects would be largest in the early years of the Super League. The reason is that some of the positive effects, such as the influx of new supporters, will still be limited in the early years. For the clubs, this will be a problem. It is therefore likely that, if a Super League emerges, media magnates and other financiers will become involved. Such entrepreneurs are used to investing first and reaping the profits many years later.

But the main conclusion is this: although the fans of big profit-driven clubs will not be in favour of the Super League, it is still possible that their owners will be.

MONEY VERSUS PASSION

Until now, we have been discussing the case in which measures are introduced to turn around the trend of increasing competitive inequality in the existing leagues. In that case, all the small clubs, as well as the big clubs that put their fans first, will be opposed to a Super League. For the big clubs that put profits first, this is less sure. They may be against a Super League in view of the loss of the fixtures in the national league, but it is also possible that they will want a Super League.

But what if no measures to improve competitive balance are adopted, so that the developments presently taking place just continue? In that case, the national leagues will become increasingly dull. As a result, the negative effects of leaving the national league will diminish. Sooner or later there will come a tipping point when, on balance, a Super League would increase the profits of the participants. At that point, the big profit-driven clubs will want to launch such a Super

League. What the other big clubs – those that aim to serve the inter-ests of their fans – will want in that scenario is less clear. If the imbal-ances in the national leagues do not become too large, these clubs may remain in favour of the old system. But if the existing leagues become very dull, the supporters of those clubs will probably want a Super League after all – which means their clubs will too.

All in all, there are big uncertainties, but the most important distinc-tion is starting to become clear. On one side are the entrepreneurs who own big clubs and are motivated by profit. Their clubs are cur-rently still playing in the existing leagues, but they also know that a Super League has the potential to be highly lucrative in the future. On the opposite side are the fans, and the clubs that represent their interests. For most fans, a Super League will be less attractive than the existing leagues, especially should the latter remain competitive or become so. It is a thrilling contest: money versus passion, drums and chanting. Which will win?

TEARING US APART

How likely is it then that a Super League will appear in the future? Let us examine the matter very closely now. The big clubs hold power in football. At present they do not seem interested in putting measures in place to help reduce competitive imbalances. This is also true for those big clubs that put the interests of supporters first. This is not surprising, because more than anything else supporters want their team to win trophies. However, the upshot is that the existing leagues are becoming ever more predictable.

It is likely that this will prompt the big profit-driven clubs to launch a Super League at some point in the future. It is unclear what the other big clubs will want to do if this happens. One possibility is that they will opt for the Super League too, because their supporters are starting to get bored with their national leagues. In this case the Super League will happen, because the big clubs have the power.

Another possibility is that the big clubs that put their fans first will not want a Super League, because their supporters continue to enjoy the national leagues despite the increase in competitive inequality (which may remain within bounds). In this case there will be a situation in which the big profit-driven clubs put forward a proposal for a Super League, while the big clubs that want to serve their fans oppose it. Would the latter be able to prevent the Super League from happening then?

There are still many big clubs that aim to serve their fans, but their numbers are gradually falling. Now and then, a club that aims to serve the fans is taken over by individuals or companies aiming for profits. As a result, among the big European clubs, the number of proponents of the Super League will increase with the passage of time. However, this will be a gradual process. In ten or twenty years' time there will still be quite a few clubs that put their fans first.

A situation could then arise where, at first, only a large proportion of the big clubs, that is, the profit-driven ones, launch a Super League with support from financiers willing to invest a lot of money in the expectation of cashing in over the long term. These clubs would then use this money to buy the best players. The other big clubs, which first and foremost want to entertain their fans, will then be at risk of becoming second-class clubs on the pitch. As this is the last thing their supporters want, all the big clubs will feel compelled to take part in the Super League, even if they would rather it didn't happen at all. The result? A Super League of all the big clubs.

Of course, the future is difficult to predict and other scenarios are also possible. One of these scenarios, for instance, could start when the debts of the Spanish clubs finally force them to cut back their expenditures on transfer fees and players' wages. As a result, the Primera División becomes less attractive. This reduces the revenues of the clubs, which in turn means that they have to cut back on new players even more, and as a result, Barcelona and Real Madrid find it increasingly difficult to beat English and German teams. Therefore, a proposal is made to merge the Spanish and Portuguese competitions, because Barcelona–Benfica raises more revenues than Barcelona–Levante. Benfica and Porto welcome this proposal, knowing they will never be the best in Europe again if they stay in the Portuguese league. And so, after many emotional debates of course, the Iberian Top Division is born.

The Italians regard this as a threat to their own clubs, but they soon recognize their geographical advantage and, as a result, the Serie A merges with the top divisions of Greece and Serbia, to start with. This move frightens even the English clubs, and it is not long before Arsenal and Liverpool play Celtic and Rangers in the Great British League. And so, step by step, a new league system emerges which may, ultimately, resemble the Super League to a large extent.

Such a system will not emerge because the fans like this more than anything else. It will emerge because of the problems of competitive inequality. With every step there will be deeply felt hesitations. Still, every single step will probably be approved by most of the fans directly affected. Spanish fans may not oppose the Iberian Top Division because it improves the chances of Spanish clubs in Europe. But their new top division will provoke reactions from other countries, and so the final effect may not be as beneficial as the Spaniards had hoped. Years later, they may reflect that it might have been better to solve their problems in other ways, so that their national competition, with its deep-rooted history, was not lost. But unfortunately, they were only thinking from their own perspective. They failed to rise above national rivalries and see the problem as a whole.

Of course, this is just one of the many possible scenarios, but in other scenarios too, similar results will occur as long as football is left to the forces of the market. In the market, every party tends to walk alone.

To conclude, it is likely that a Super League system, or a league system that resembles a Super League to a large extent, will eventually come about – especially if the authorities do nothing to intervene, because in principle, the authorities, and in this case the EU, have even more power than the big clubs. If the EU does not want there to be a Super League, it can impose measures that will make the existing competitions less predictable. This will reduce the chances of a Super League happening. Even then, the big clubs could still decide to set up such a competition. In that case, the EU could simply prohibit the Super League, for example, on the grounds that this is what football fans want.

But how likely is that? We are talking about the EU here. Wasn't that the same organization that eroded the foreigner rule and emasculated the transfer system? That put its own principles above people and above sports? Can Brussels really be football fans' best hope?

6

THE CHALLENGE

AN EVER LARGER WORLD

In these modern times we have access to music, movies and ideas from all over the world. We take a holiday in Turkey or admire the Taj Mahal in India. Our clothes come from far-away countries that can produce them cheaply. Globalization has many other effects, including negative ones of course. We cannot discuss all this here. However, one effect deserves attention: the waning powers of national governments.

In the 1960s, national governments still had large powers. For instance, they could set the rate of the corporate tax, or in other words, the tax on profits, at the level they desired. There were left-wing governments that increased the rate, because profits do not usually go to the poorest. Some right-wing governments lowered it, arguing that profit-making entrepreneurs should be encouraged, since they generate employment. And because national governments had the ability to change the corporate tax rate, and to introduce many other telling measures, national elections mattered and democracies flourished.

At present, many on the left still consider a high corporate tax to be fair. Even so, in the Netherlands, for instance, its rate has fallen sharply in recent years, with the agreement of the social democratic party. The reason was that rates in other countries had gone even lower. As a result, the Dutch government – including the social democrats – feared that firms would leave the country if the Dutch rate remained unchanged. But every country thinks the same way, leading to lower corporate taxes everywhere. We are in a 'race to the bottom', in which competition between countries not only forces governments to cut the corporate tax, but also to mitigate many other policies such as, for instance, regulation of working conditions. Faced with firms that can choose to go elsewhere when a country introduces policies they don't like, the power of national governments has decreased.

This also makes national politics less interesting. In the Netherlands, for instance, there are no longer heated debates about the corporate tax. The loss of debates such as this one has contributed to the lower turnout on election days.

A similar story holds for football. Of course, national governments can still be helpful here, for example, in the fight against hooliganism. However, many of the measures that could help the sport cannot be introduced by one country in isolation. One example is a ban on pay TV for football broadcasts. If such a ban were introduced by one country only, this would mean that the football fans of that country would be able to watch the televised matches for free. But it would also reduce the revenues of the clubs, so that good players would move abroad – which would be bad for the fans. Other measures introduced by a single country, such as a progressive social levy, will not work well for similar reasons. Thus, they cannot be an issue during national elections, which is a pity, since a debate about football could help make elections much more interesting for fans.

THE EUROPEAN UNION

In 1957, exactly one hundred years after the foundation of Sheffield FC by Nathaniel Creswick and William Prest, the EU was founded. At the start, the new organization primarily promoted free trade across national borders, and this had a big impact on economic life. Firms were no longer protected by national boundaries and faced serious competition from elsewhere in the EU. Some firms did not survive the competition, but the more efficient ones grew in size. These firms produced good-quality, inexpensive products, so that economic welfare improved. At present, many EU firms are still very competitive, and in some cases, they are better than American or Asian firms. Indeed, the European market has helped prepare our firms for the challenges of globalization. The EU has done other good things too, and some bad things as well, of course, but there isn't scope to talk about that here. Some points, however, deserve special attention.

As discussed before, national governments have lost power in the face of firms that can move across borders. Here, the EU has something to offer. For instance, it could ensure that corporate tax is harmonized across the EU so that firms no longer move from one EU country to another for the purpose of paying lower taxes. Of course, they could still threaten to go to America if the harmonized tax rate rose too far, but relatively few firms would make such a drastic move. With harmonization, the corporate tax would be on the political agenda again, as it would be possible to discuss how high the EU rate should be. Good. If we want our governments to build schools and roads, we need to discuss all possible ways to finance them. And then we might have elections with, hopefully, heated debates.

To be sure, the Union should not pursue policies that can also be pursued at the national level. It is a good thing that this principle has always been given a prominent place in the European Treaties. Unfortunately, what's put into practice is often different. For instance, EU money is being used to fund projects that help 'poor' Dutch regions. One such project happens to be close to my home: a well-designed bridge across a canal for cyclists and walkers. It is intended to promote tourism in the beautiful region of Twente. And indeed, the view from the bridge is great. But still, why should English and Greek taxpayers help fund this project when the Dutch taxpayers, who are among the richer ones in the Union, could fully finance it themselves? Let the Dutch solve the Dutch problems. In thinking this way, some of the EU policies could easily be abandoned.

But the Union should be active in cases where it really has something to add. The harmonization of the corporate tax rate represents one such case. The policies for football represent another one. And in many other policy fields EU policies can be useful too. That is to say, if the EU were a democratic and well-functioning organization. But is it?

A MAJOR DEMOCRACY PROBLEM

Many people like their own country and spend time thinking and talking about its future. Many either like their country's prime minister, as a politician or as a person, or they might be completely fed up with him or her. However, few people are really interested in the EU, and few know the EU politicians well. This is a problem, since a democracy needs informed voters who hold politicians accountable for their deeds.

Most people agree that the EU has something to offer in principle, in some areas at least. But, partly because the EU is not very popular, most national governments have been hesitant in handing over powers to the Union. This has resulted in complicated bureaucratic compromises. In many policy fields, a large number of different players – both from the EU and the individual member states – have a say. And when many have a say, few can be held responsible. In such a situation it is difficult for voters, and for politicians too, to have influence and to control what's going on.

The fact that democratic control is often weak in the EU due to too much bureaucracy is a valid argument for reducing the powers of the EU in some fields. For instance, the EU has very large budgets for agricultural and regional development policies, but when politicians and bureaucrats get large budgets there is always a danger that the money is not used well – which implies that there needs to be good control. However, control in the EU tends to be weak, and therefore there is a valid reason to reduce the budgets for agricultural and regional development policies.

However, this kind of argument is less important when it comes to the policy of harmonization of the corporate tax rate across the Union. After all, even with harmonization, the revenues of this tax will still go to the individual member states, so that misuse of funds by EU bureaucrats is not an issue here. In addition, once there is agreement that all countries should have a tax rate of, say, 20 per cent minimum, no civil servant will be required to ensure that all countries comply with the rule. The press will take care of that. So there are no serious problems of control at the EU level with regard to this measure, and bureaucratic problems will also be few regarding a number of other EU policies.

This also applies to the policy measures for football advocated in this book. It has been proposed that the EU should ban subsidies for professional clubs more strictly, and that it should introduce a ban on pay TV and install a progressive social levy which forces clubs to invest in social projects. In addition, the EU could renew the transfer system and reinstate the foreigner rule. Now, once there is political agreement on these policies, it can basically be left to the football authorities and the press to control the new rules. For instance, no civil servants will be needed to maintain the pay-TV ban; the press will take care of that too. Maintaining the renewed transfer and foreigner rules can be left to the football authorities; history shows they are very good at such things. And, as argued earlier, UEFA's FFP system can be used to ban subsidies. In addition, the obligation for clubs to invest in social projects that are funded by the social levy can also become part of that system. Admittedly, UEFA will need some help from government to make it work well, but with smart rules relatively few civil servants will be needed for that, so that the costs of the policy can remain small compared to its benefits.

So, yes, there are democratic and bureaucratic problems, but this does not mean there shouldn't be any EU policies. Quite the contrary, especially when it comes to football.

ALL THE WAY FROM BRUSSELS TO CELTIC PARK

With the EU democracy being weak, and control of politicians and civil servants insufficient, lobbyists have much influence in Brussels. This may help explain why the EU has often helped the big companies. Banks, for instance, have received much aid during recent years. Of course, there was a good reason for this: the economy would have collapsed if the big banks had gone broke. However, the aid has often been quite generous, while the EU has been slow to regulate the banks strictly enough to ensure that they need not be rescued (again) in future. This is not to deny that there have been improvements, but fundamental changes are still not in sight.

Examples such as this one raise questions. Do big companies perhaps represent a rather too successful lobby in Brussels? Is this about the powerlessness of the European Parliament? Do those in power really want the people to get more involved with the EU, and to strengthen the EU democracy?

José Manuel Barroso has been one of the most powerful men in Europe for nearly ten years. He became the President of the European Commission in 2004. At the time of writing this book he still occupies that position, although he is expected to leave in October 2014. Unfortunately, you probably do not know this powerful man as well as you know your own national leaders.

Barroso has always said that the EU is beneficial for the people. When opponents have criticized this view, he and his fellow Commissioners have often reacted by saying that the criticism meant that they had failed to explain clearly why the EU is so beneficial, and that they should try to improve their explanation. Whatever one may think of such a reaction, it is certainly difficult for a European leader to reach out to the people he is supposed to lead. After all, few citizens are really interested in the EU to begin with.

Barroso has spent much of his time in Brussels meeting other politicians and civil servants. Lobbyists have also tried to take up much of his time. Indeed, he has been a very busy man, but despite this, he always wanted to explain the benefits of the EU to the people, as well as its problems, of course. Good. Let us hope that the new president, appointed in October 2014, has the same kind of attitude.

So let us pose some questions about football, so that the new president can explain the views of the European Commission. Why is it that the EU has eroded the foreigner rule and the transfer system? Is the European Treaty a holy grail, or is the EU capable of learning from its own mistakes and changing the law when necessary?

And what is it that has made the EU do so little to prevent the rise of pay TV, so that many people now have to pay heavily to watch football matches that could easily be broadcast for free? What is the view of the President on the bigger clubs getting ever more chances to win the main trophies? Will the new European Commission have the same policy as the old one and allow football, which owes its soul and its popularity to the work of volunteers, to be dominated by money? Why has the EU, the only power that can bring football back to the people, done so little here?

So, does the President of the European Commission really want to explain the European ideals to the people? And would the President dare to come, all the way from Brussels, to meet the heirs of Brother Walfrid down in Celtic Park?

WILL YOU WALK ALONE?

The choice before us is really very clear. There are two possible scenarios to choose between. In the first, the existing developments largely continue undisturbed. Our governments do not act, except to curb excesses such as transfers of young children perhaps. Apart from this, the big clubs decide what happens because they have the power within professional football.

As long as the current league system continues to exist, these clubs make little effort to reduce competitive imbalances. Therefore, the imbalances become even more pronounced. The big clubs in particular earn even more. And more clubs come into the hands of owners who are looking to turn a profit. The increasing competitive imbalances ultimately lead the big clubs to set up a Super League. The sixty clubs, at most, taking part in it will no longer compete in their own national leagues. For all kinds of reasons, the Super League boosts the profits of its participants, and that is precisely what many of the new club owners want. Football fans are faced with higher prices. Certainly at the outset, some clubs in the Super League are still associations or foundations. As long as they perform well, most can remain that way. But if such a club performs poorly for some time, it is likely to be taken over by an entrepreneur. Eventually, football will take on an American aspect.

Of course, the future is difficult to predict, and at the level of details the developments may differ from those outlined above. In any case, the first scenario implies that the biggest European clubs will play one another more often and they will divide all the important prizes among themselves in the end.

In the second scenario, the EU actively intervenes. In order to reduce competitive imbalances, it introduces a progressive social levy on the amount a club pays out in players' wages, and a pay-TV ban for all important matches. These measures not only reduce inequality, they also have other benefits: clubs invest more in social projects and football becomes cheaper for the fans. If the social levy is sufficiently progressive, no other measures will be needed to increase uncertainty of outcome. Nevertheless, the EU might also allow, or even stimulate, the clubs to introduce a new foreigner rule, whilst a strict transfer system might also be brought back. Apart from making the competitions less predictable, the last two measures also have some other benefits, such as supporters seeing some more of their fellow countrymen playing for their club. But back to uncertainty of outcome. This increases due to all four measures. The net result will be to make the advent of a Super League less likely. At the same time, the possibility remains that a number of rich clubs and entrepreneurs may still want to launch a Super League. If this were in danger of happening, the EU would simply prohibit it.

Finally, the EU could prevent too many clubs coming into the hands of profit-driven owners, for example by promoting rules such as the German one that private investors are not allowed to own more than 49 per cent of the shares of a club. But in view of the other measures, this might no longer really be necessary; after all, those measures in themselves force the clubs to be socially responsible. All in all, in this second scenario, football will get closer to its European, social roots.

Most football fans would probably choose the second scenario. But if the authorities are not sure, they could poll the fans in order to investigate their preferences. The EU and UEFA could even organize a vote among all fans who belong to an official supporters organization, asking them which measures they would like to be introduced. All fans would then play a part in the people's game again. Wouldn't that be the real theatre of dreams?

Back to reality. Were such a poll taken, my prediction is that the majority of fans would want the authorities to promote the second scenario.

But will the EU do what the people want? To date, it has mainly favoured the free market, to the detriment of football. In fact, even aside from football, the EU is very far removed from the people. It is not really democratic. And there are many other things wrong with the EU. But the EU is the only body that still has the power to bring football back to the people.

That would require a drastic change of course. If the Union really wants to help the football fans, it must confront the rich football entrepreneurs and the media tycoons – even though these tycoons, through their newspapers and television stations, can make life very difficult for politicians they take a dislike to. So none of this will be easy. But it can be done, at least if there are politicians who are prepared to fight for the fans. Whatever you think of the EU, it is football's best hope.

This is a chance for the Union to show what it stands for. Is it an organization unwilling to defy the rich entrepreneurs and the media tycoons? Or will it use its power to give football a social face again, and a European one at that? For now, the answer is hidden in the shadows. And so, at the end of the book, there's no golden sky and no sweet, silver song of a lark. After all these words and phrases, the most important question still remains unanswered: will the fans walk alone?

INDEX